A–Z

OF

WREXHAM

PLACES - PEOPLE - HISTORY

Christopher Davies

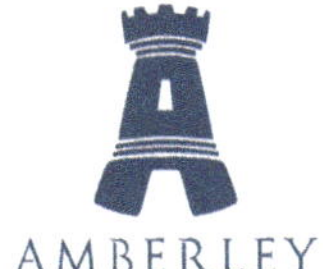

AMBERLEY

First published 2023

Amberley Publishing
The Hill, Stroud, Gloucestershire, GL5 4EP
www.amberley-books.com

Copyright © Christopher Davies, 2023

The right of Christopher Davies to be identified
as the Author of this work has been asserted in
accordance with the Copyrights, Designs and
Patents Act 1988.

ISBN 978 1 4456 9905 9 (print)
ISBN 978 1 4456 9906 6 (ebook)

British Library Cataloguing in Publication Data.
A catalogue record for this book is available from
the British Library.

Origination by Amberley Publishing.
Printed in Great Britain.

Contents

Introduction

When asked to compile an A–Z of a Welsh town like Wrexham, the first question that springs to mind is, 'Is this going to be based on the English or the Welsh alphabet?' Given the modest size of the book, it was fairly clear that, on this occasion, the English alphabet would prevail.

The aim of this small book is to give visitors and those new to the town something of a feel for Wrexham and the surrounding area. I have chosen to write about the area of Wrexham County Borough, rather than concentrate on the town, to the exclusion of other interesting places in the locality which have, one way or another, impacted the area. However, I must own up to straying just outside of the county borough on occasion, in order to provide a more complete picture.

Writing in 2008, the author Simon Jenkins described Wrexham as a 'dejected and devastated town'. One could argue that this was rather a harsh comment, but on reflection we can see how a visitor might get such an impression of the town. The fact that not all visitors were as negative as Simon Jenkins demonstrates that towns are constantly changing and developing. Samuel Johnson, for example, thought Wrexham 'a busy, extensive and well-built town' and, in 1839, the author and cleric Revd William Bingley remarked that 'Wrexham was of such size and consequence as to have occasionally obtained the appellation of the metropolis of North Wales.' Perhaps the difference between the latter description and that of Jenkins is reflective of the way in which Wrexham has changed and developed in the last 150 years.

Today Wrexham is, as Shakespeare might have put it, 'a vain shadow of its former self'. The heavy industry is long gone and the extensive rail network is no more. The coal industry, which provided employment for many hundreds, finally disappeared with the closure of Bersham Colliery in 1986. Yet not all of the past is lost, despite some questionable twentieth-century planning decisions, which have seen the demise of many older buildings. At least one correspondent writing to the *Wrexham Leader* had noted that 'our heritage of historical buildings are disappearing at an alarming rate. Future historians in the Wrexham district will look on the 1960s as the most destructive decade of the century.' However, there is still much in the area to enlighten us about its history. Within the Wrexham County Borough area, for example, there are some 1,040 listed buildings. Wrexham itself is certainly one of those towns where one needs to look above ground-floor level in order to spot some of the more unusual aspects of the town's architecture.

There is evidence of Roman occupation in the area, and as recently as 2020, a Roman villa was discovered at Rossett near Wrexham. Wrexham itself is possibly an Anglo-Saxon foundation and it is situated in an area where control frequently passed between the English and the Welsh. There is record of a castle in 1261, and it is thought that this was a motte-and-bailey structure standing in the area of Erddig Park. Leyland confirmed its commercial importance in the 1530s 'as the only market town in Welsh Malor'.

Historically, Wrexham was part of Denbighshire, but became part of Clwyd in 1974. Wrexham County Borough was created on 1 April 1966, the borough status having been inherited from the town of Wrexham, which had been granted it some 150 years ago. Although it is the largest town in North Wales, Wrexham has never achieved city status. The town has applied for city status on three occasions: at the millennium and on the occasions of the Queen's Golden and Diamond jubilees. Despite being North Wales' largest town, in March 2012, Wrexham missed out to the very much smaller St Asaph, which was granted city status. However, city status was finally achieved in May 2022 as part of the celebrations for the Queen's Platinum Jubilee. Prior to the award of city status, one councillor remarked that city status would enable Wrexham to 'fulfil its role as the major urban centre and heart of North Wales'. In 2021, it was announced that Wrexham was bidding to become UK City of Culture in 2025. However, on this occasion the accolade went to the city of Bradford. On 9 December 2022, King Charles III and Queen Camilla visited Wrexham to formally confirm its city status.

Readers seeking a more in-depth view of Wrexham's history would do well to consult *The Encyclopaedia of Wrexham* by W. Alister Williams or A. H. Dodd's *A History of Wrexham, Denbighshire*. Rex Christiansen's *Forgotten Railways of North and Mid Wales* is useful in providing an overview of railway development in the area.

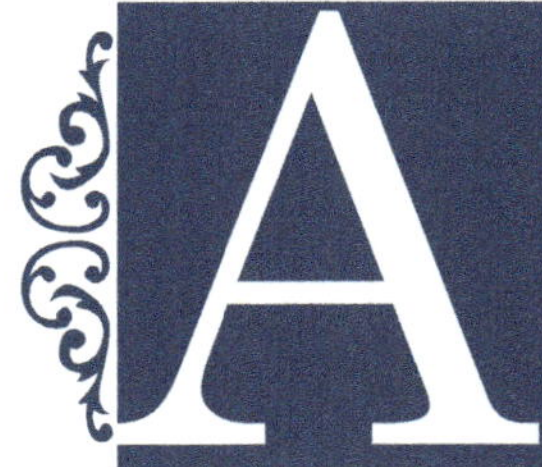

Acton Hall and Park

Acton Hall was the seat of the Jeffreys family from the seventeenth century. The family's prosperity was founded by John Jeffreys, an Anglesey circuit judge. Probably the most famous member of the family was George Jeffreys, the notorious hanging judge. The hall was rebuilt by Sir Griffith Jeffreys between 1687 and 1695. However, by 1747, the Jeffreys family had sold the hall, which was then owned successively by Philip Egerton and Ellis Young, before being purchased by Sir Foster Cunliffe, 3rd Baronet. The new owner almost immediately set about improving the house with the addition of a new wing and laying out the park. The lake, which is a central feature of the park, was laid out at this time. After the death of the 6th Baronet in 1917, the property was purchased by Sir Bernard Oppenheimer, who set up a diamond cutting school and workshops to train ex-servicemen. However, the scheme closed after Sir Bernard's death in 1921.

In 1920, Wrexham Council bought over 60 acres of the estate for a new housing scheme. The hall was purchased by Alderman William Ashton, who planned to turn it into a technical school. However, the plan never came to fruition, and for the next few years, the building was used as a store. In 1939, the house and park was requisitioned

Acton Park Gates. These imposing gates to the Acton Park estate now serve to frame the modern housing behind them.

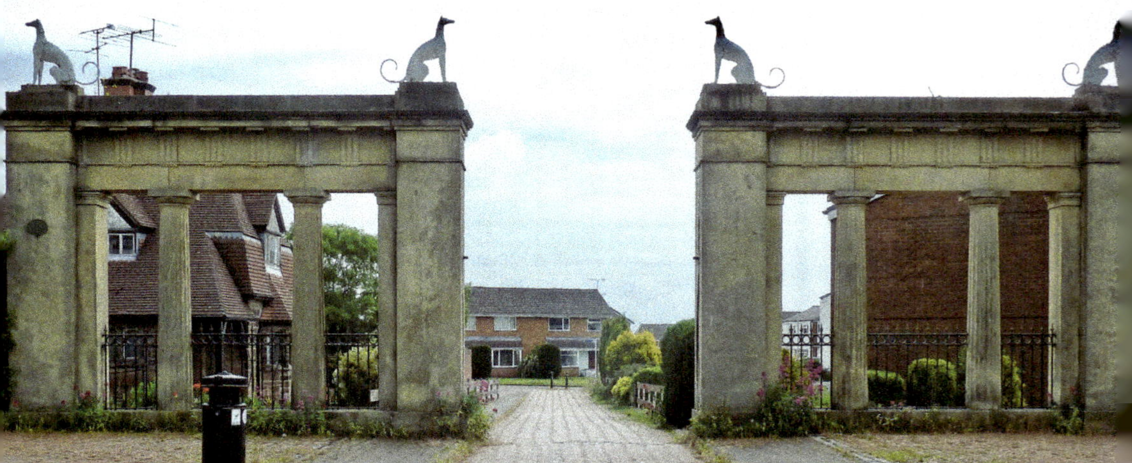

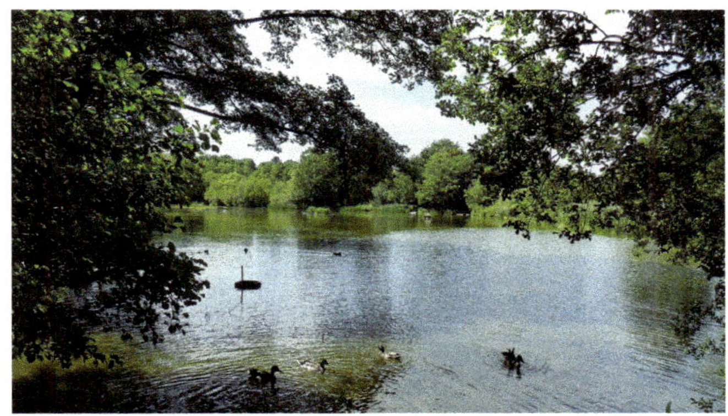

Acton Park lake. One of the focal points of the park is the lake, which is well used by local fishermen.

by the War Office for military use, with officers being billeted in the house and other ranks in Nissan huts in the grounds. A number of different regiments were billeted in the park and, in 1943, American troops moved in.

By 1945, the house was not in a particularly good condition, and William Ashton gifted the house and the park to Wrexham Borough Council. In 1954, the house was demolished; all that remains as a reminder today are the gates to the park.

The park itself, however, continues as an essential part of the local area. Many of the mature trees in the park are those planted when the park was laid out by Sir Foster Cunliffe in 1785.

Aqueducts

Pontcysyllte

Sir Water Scott described Pontcysyllte Aqueduct as 'the greatest work of art he had ever seen'. More recently, it has been described as a 'marriage of elegance and engineering'. Today, in an age where mega structures are almost commonplace, it is too easy to underestimate the significance of Pontcysyllte Aqueduct as one of the wonders of its age and a pioneer in the use of cast iron as a building material.

Envisaged as the central section of the Ellesmere Canal, it was originally intended to cross the Dee Valley at a much lower level, with a series of locks taking the canal down to an aqueduct 50 feet above the River Dee. However, following the success of the Longdon-on-Tern Aqueduct, Thomas Telford conceived the idea of carrying the canal across the valley at full height, in an iron trough mounted on a series of stone pillars. The idea was approved by William Jessop and work began in 1795.

The eighteen sandstone pillars were quarried at Cefn Mawr and transported to the site, where it would have been cut and dressed. The pillars taper from 6.4 metres at the base to 5.1 metres at the top. The ironwork for the trough was cast by William Hazeldine at his foundries in Shrewsbury and Cefn Mawr. A lesson learned from Longdon-on-Tern was to make the trough slightly wider and to cantilever the towpath out from the side to allow for the displacement of water.

Chirk

Chirk Aqueduct was begun in June 1796, later than Pontcysyllte, but it was finished well before it in 1801. There were two reasons for this. Firstly, it was easier to construct and its completion, including the tunnel, up to Froncysyllte added another 4 miles to the canal. This allowed for the easier movement of coal from Black Park Colliery. Designed by Telford, the aqueduct has ten spans each of 40 feet. It is interesting that cast iron was only used for the bed of the aqueduct and masonry, quarried at nearby Pond Faen, for the sides, whereas at Longdon-on-Tern and Pontcysyllte, complete iron troughs were used. Running parallel with the aqueduct, and standing some 30 feet above it, is Henry Robertson's railway viaduct of 1848. At the end of the aqueduct is Chirk Tunnel, which was one of the first tunnels in the UK to have a towpath. The English-Welsh border runs across the middle of the aqueduct.

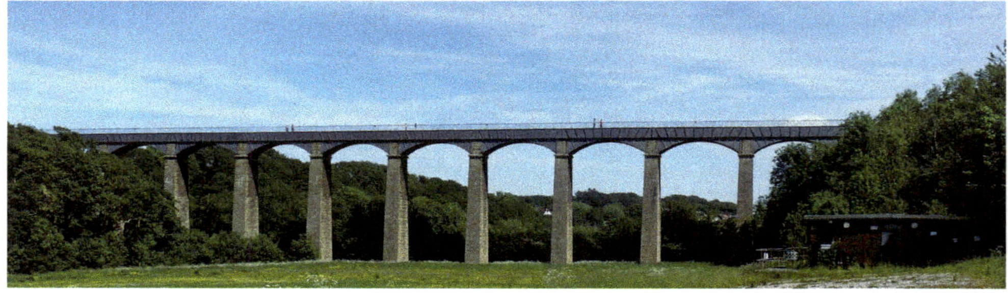

Above: Pontcysyllte Aqueduct, built by Thomas Telford and William Jessop between 1795 and 1805 to carry the Ellesmere Canal over the Dee Valley.

Below: Chirk Aqueduct was also designed by Thomas Telford and built between 1796 and 1801.

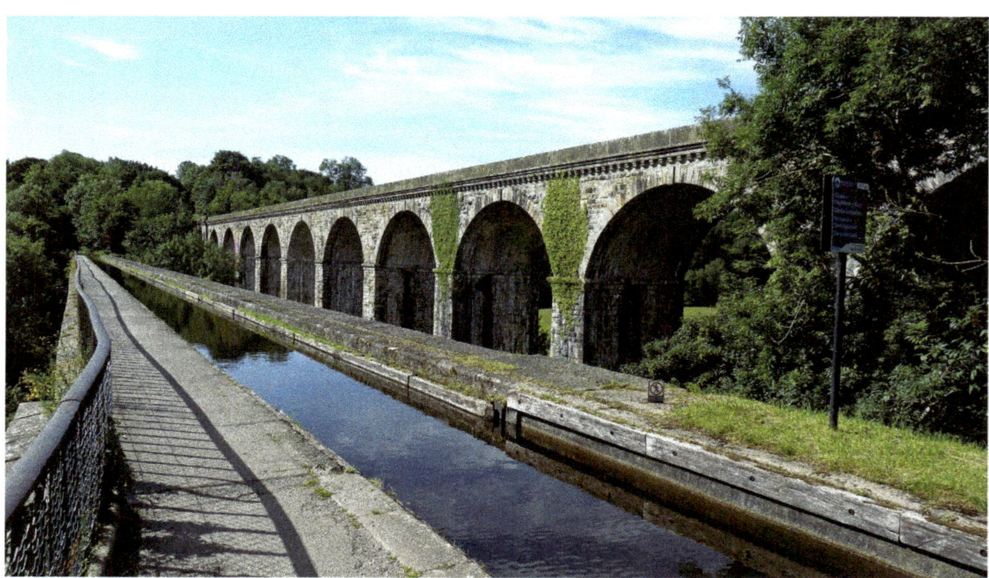

Bersham Ironworks

Charles Lloyd began smelting at Bersham in the early eighteenth century, but being unable to make it pay, gave up the furnace in 1726. For the next twenty-seven years, the furnace was run by a number of other iron masters until being taken over by Isaac Wilkinson in 1753. It was Isaac's son John whose name would be forever associated with Bersham. Isaac Wilinson gave up the Bersham business after about eight years, and a new company was formed by his sons John and William. From the outset, John was the leader in this venture, having gained a wide experience in the ironworks in the Midlands, while William had remained at Bersham.

Although the Seven Years' War was nearing its end, Wilkinson pushed ahead with the munitions side of the business. The works were reconstructed and cannon, grenades and shells were produced in large quantities. The war ended in 1763, and Wilkinson began to diversify his business interests, buying up corn and fulling mills, with a view to controlling the rivers that supplied his power. He also began to experiment with improved ways of boring cannon. Hitherto, cannon had been cast in one piece with a core. Since the whole thing was cast, there were often imperfections in the casting, which could have catastrophic results when the cannon was fired. In 1774–75, Wilkinson invented a cannon-boring machine which produced a safer and more accurate piece of ordinance.

Wilkinson's cannon-lathe also found more peaceful uses. James Watt and Matthew Boulton found that Wilkinson's lathe would produce cylinders 'with that truth and exactness we require'. For the next twenty years, most of the engines supplied by Boulton and Watt had their cylinders made at one of Wilkinson's works. For a number of reasons, not least of which was the need to buy-in coal and iron stone, John Wilkinson was becoming dissatisfied with the Bersham works and, in 1792, he purchased the Brymbo Hall estate. Within two years of buying the estate two blast furnaces and a boring mill were built and coal shafts were being sunk.

The Brymbo site had a long and chequered history as an iron and steel works. Along with the rest of the steel industry, it was nationalised in 1967, becoming part of the British Steel Corporation. The steelworks closed for good in 1990. Wilkinson's No. 1 blast furnace is extant, and it is hoped that this will be preserved.

There are still buildings on the original Bersham site, including the Corn Mill building, which may have been one of John Wilkinson's boring mills. There is also a striking octagonal building that must have played an important role in the ironworks. It is featured in the 1780s drawing of the works surrounded by smaller buildings. In 1983, the Heritage Centre was opened just along the road from the Bersham site. This is the central point for information about the Clywedog Valley and has exhibitions about the industrial history of the area.

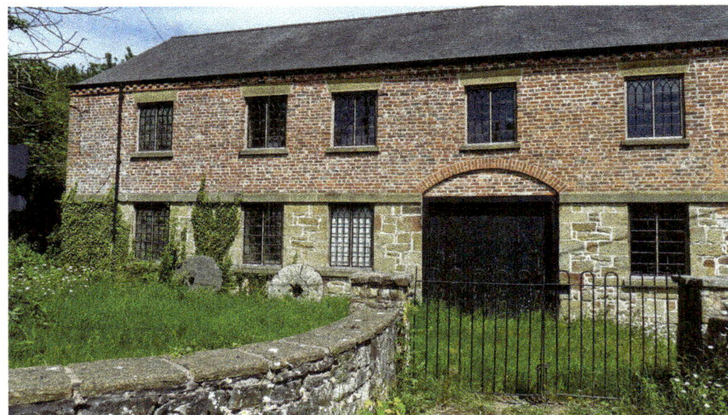

Left: Bersham Ironworks, one of the cradles of the Industrial Revolution.

Below: Bersham Ironworks. This octagonal building was where cannon were cast.

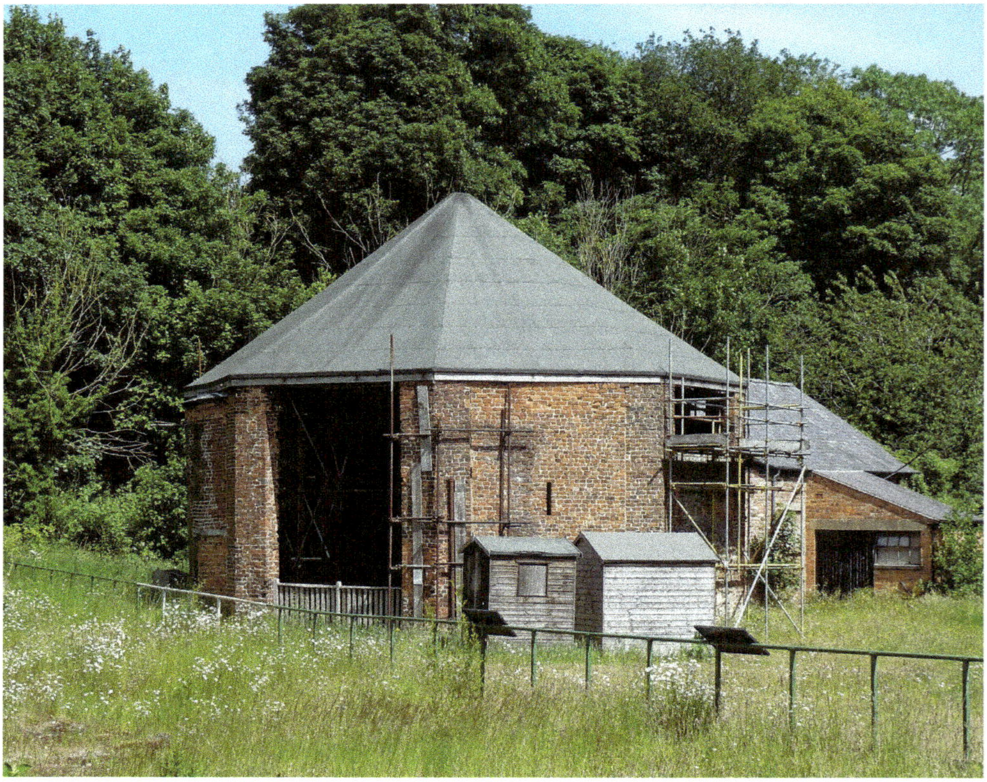

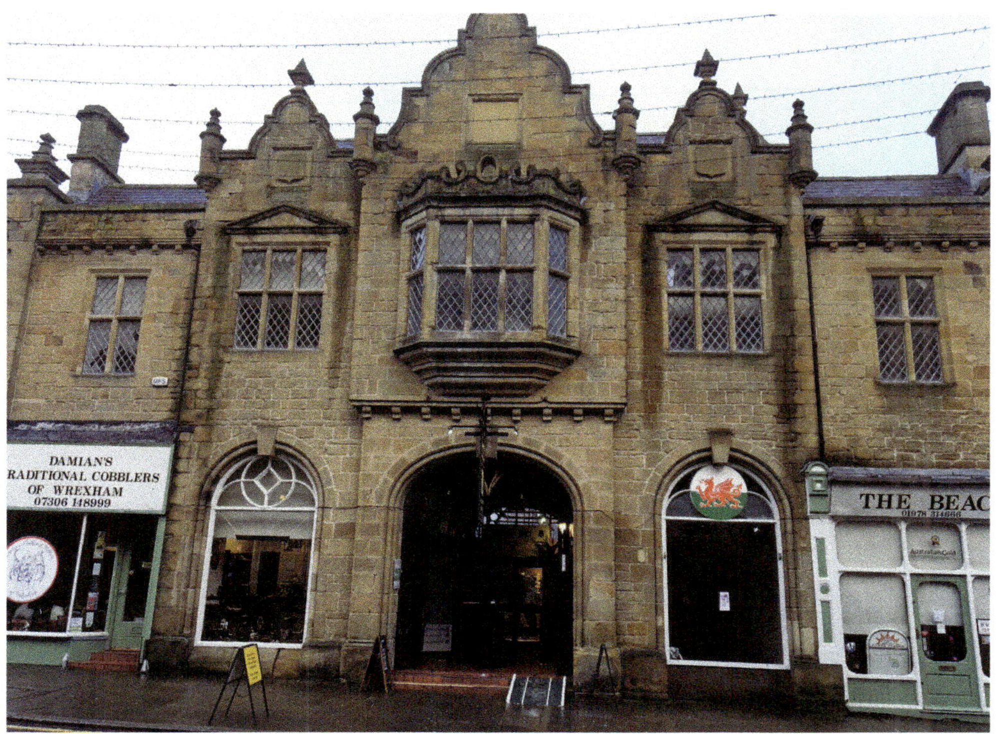

The Butchers' Market in Wrexham High Street. It was designed by Thomas Penson and opened in March 1848.

Butchers' Market

Designed by Thomas Penson, the Butchers' Market was the first of Wrexham's three indoor markets. It opened in March 1848, having been built by the Wrexham Market Hall Company. Prior to this, butchers had open stalls in High Street, Church Street and Abbot Street.

Bellevue Park (Parciau)

The idea of a local park was first made in 1876, but it was some years before suitable land was acquired, and work on the development of the park did not start until 1910. Bellevue Park is known locally as Parciau. The park was intended to commemorate the jubilee of the town's incorporation. There is a natural amphitheatre in the south-eastern area of the park where, in the summer months, regular concerts and live music events take place. No Edwardian park would be complete without its bandstand, and Bellevue Park has a particularly fine one. It had deteriorated over the years, but was refurbished in 1973. During the Second World War, the park was given over to the production of food for local canteens. The park was extensively refurbished in 1999, and as well as providing some excellent tree-lined walks, it now has a children's play area, bowling green, basketball court and tennis courts.

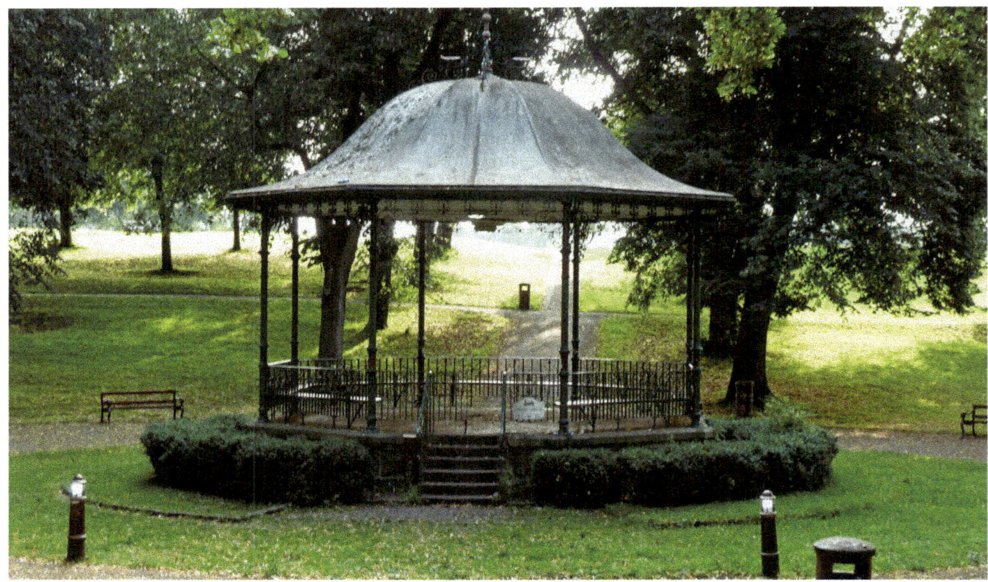

The Parciau (Bellevue Park). Work on the park started in 1911 and was completed in 1920. The bandstand dates from 1918. The park was refurbished by Wrexham County Borough Council in 1999.

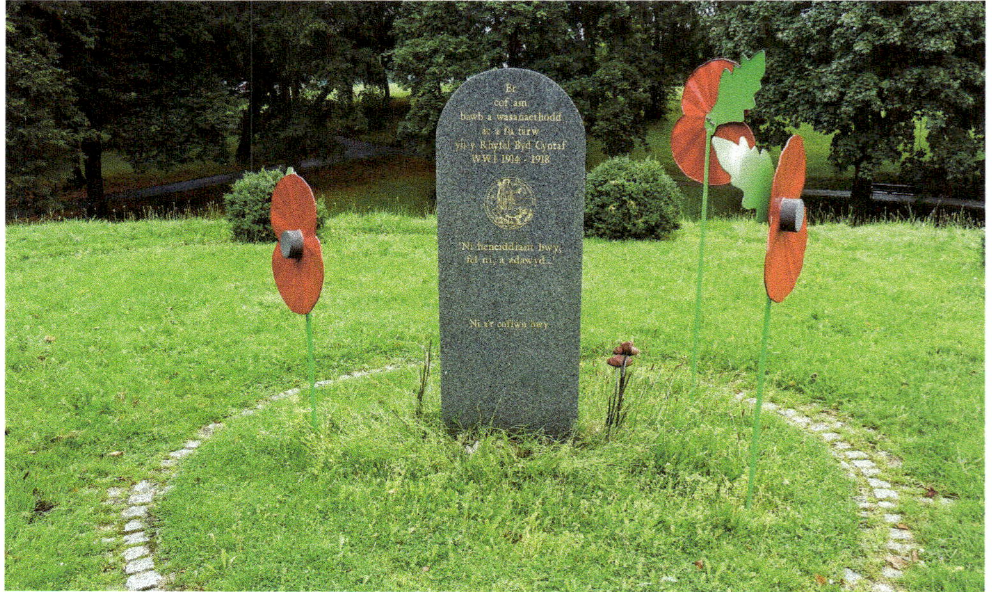

The Bellevue Park memorial to those who fell in the First World War.

Chirk Castle

Chirk Castle lies 1 mile west of Chirk. It was built by Roger Mortimer de Chirk in 1295, as part of Edward I's chain of castles in North Wales and guards the entrance to the Ceiriog Valley. The castle was bought by Sir Thomas Myddleton I in 1593. His son, also Thomas Myddleton, fought for Parliament during the English Civil War, but supported the Royalist cause during the Cheshire Rising of 1659. The castle had been seized by the Royalists in 1643, and was held by them for the next three years. Although Sir Thomas was active in Parliaments cause, his forces took Newtown and Montgomery Castle, he clearly drew the line at attacking his own castle. However, the castle was besieged by Parliament in 1659, causing considerable damage. The Myddleton family remained at Chirk until just before the First World War when the castle was leased to Thomas Scott-Ellis, 8th Baron Howard de Waldon, who remained there until after the Second World War, when the Myddleton family moved back to the castle. The castle has been in the care of the National Trust since 1981.

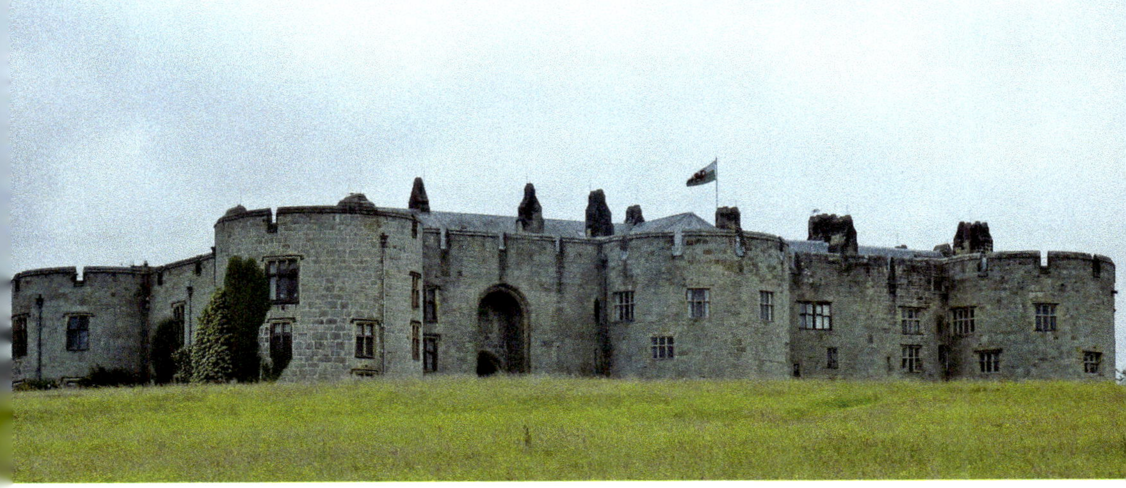

Chirk Castle, built by Roger Mortimer de Chirk in 1295 and home of the Myddleton family since 1593, is now in the care of the National Trust.

Cemetery

Wrexham's Victorian cemetery is situated in Ruabon Road. Opened in 1876, the layout was designed by the then borough surveyor, Yeo Strachan. The chapel, which is Grade II listed, was designed by John Turner. While it may seem strange today, the cemetery was laid out as a garden cemetery for the recreation of the people of Wrexham. Given the Victorian obsession with death, this would not have seemed at all unusual. Since its opening, the cemetery has expanded twice from its original 10 acres to cover an area of 7.2 hectares. There have been some 37,000 burials in the cemetery.

Coal Mines

The north-east Wales coalfield stretched from Prestatyn in the north to Oswestry in the south, and coal mining in the Wrexham area can be traced back to the fifteenth century, although at that stage it was little more than surface digging. Possibly the oldest colliery in the Wrexham area was Black Park, Chirk, which appears to have been in existence by 1653. The Industrial Revolution of the late eighteenth and nineteenth centuries stimulated the need for coal, and many new pits were opened in the area. Although it is possible to trace some 92 mines in the Wrexham area, many were quite short-lived. At the peak of coal production in the Wrexham area, there were thirty-eight different collieries employing some 18,000 people and producing

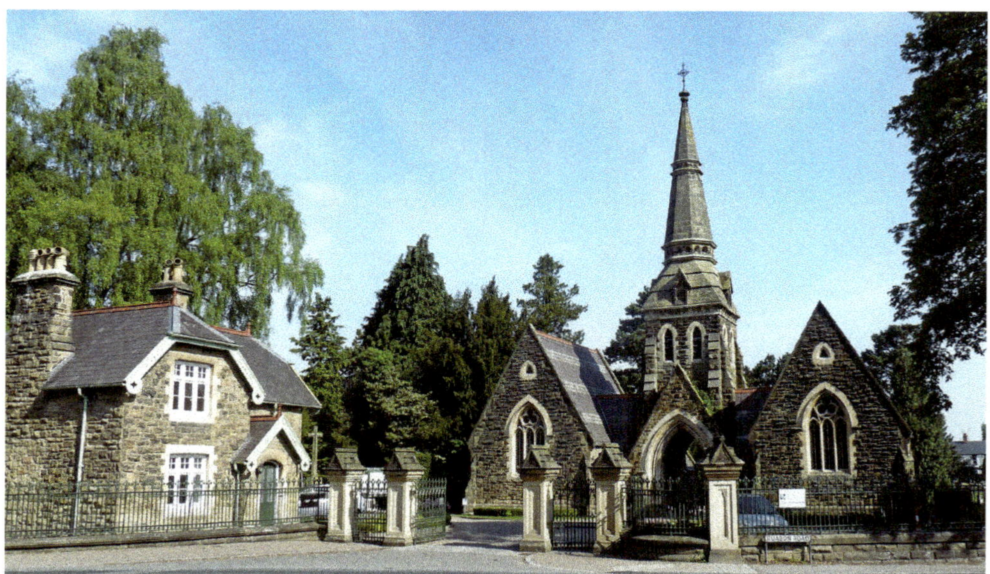

Wrexham Cemetery, opened in 1876 and designed by Yeo Strachan, the then borough surveyor. The cemetery originally consisted of just 10 acres to the rear of the chapel. It was designed as a 'garden cemetery' for the passive recreation of the people of Wrexham.

coal totalling 2.5 million tons annually. At the end of the Second World War, the coal industry was in a poor state and, in 1948, the post-war government brought it under nationalisation. Although this brought about more investment in the industry, the overall reliance on coal as a fuel diminished and there were a large number of pit closures in the 1960s, 1970s and 1980s. Bersham Colliery at Rhostyllen was the last active colliery, and brought its last coal to the surface in 1986. The Bersham engine house and winding gear still remain as one of the few visible reminders of an industry that had lasted in the area for over 300 years.

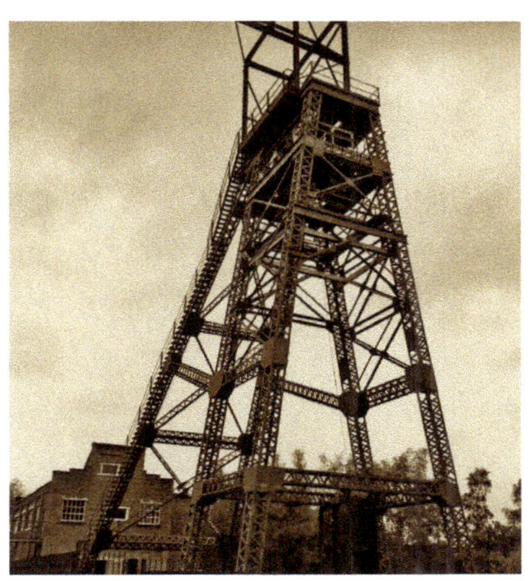

Bersham Colliery was the last of the local collieries to close when it brought its last coal to the surface in 1986. The winding house and head gear are the last tangible reminders of an industry that once employed some 18,000 people in the area. The Bersham site is now in the care of the North Wales Miners Association Trust.

This statue of a miner was erected in the Miners Memorial Garden at St Martin's in 2018 to mark fifty years since the closure of Ifton coal mine. Although Ifton Colliery was not in Wrexham County Borough, the mine was very much part of the Welsh coalfield.

Croesnewydd Hall

Built in 1696, probably by Peter Ellice, this late seventeenth-century hall now forms part of Wrexham Technology Park. It is almost certainly the second building on this site, and is an early example of brick building in this part of North Wales. The hall was purchased by Clwyd County Council in 1984, and underwent extensive restoration. The hall is now in use as offices.

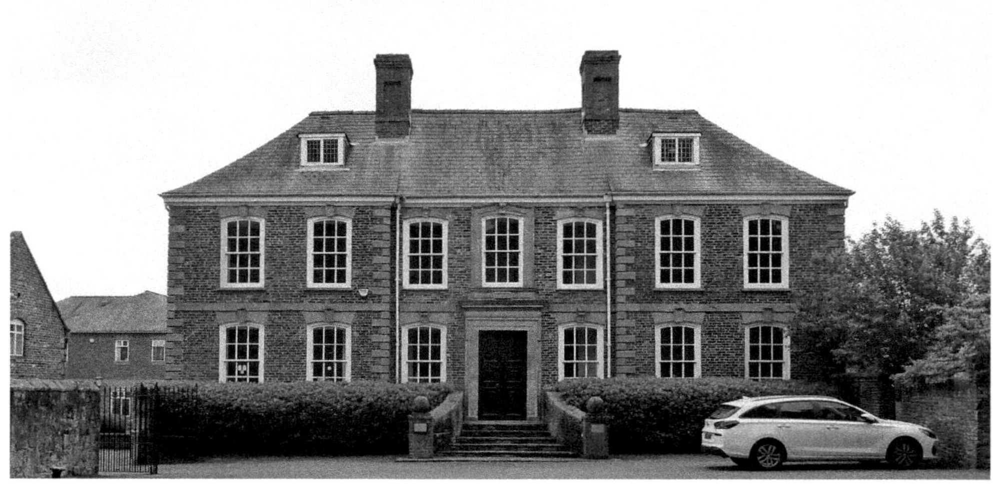

Croesnewydd Hall. Dating from 1696, the hall was built by Peter Ellice and replaced a much earlier building.

Davies Brothers

Robert and John Davies were the sons of Hugh Davies, who was a smith working at Croes Foel forge, Bersham, in the late seventeenth and early eighteenth centuries. Both sons became smiths and are particularly renowned for their wrought-iron work, several examples of which still survive in the area. Pevsner described the Davies brothers' work as 'miraculous'. Of particular note in the Wrexham area are the gates to Chirk Castle and the gates into St Giles' churchyard. Other examples, slightly further afield, include the gates of Ruthin Church and the golden gates of Eaton Hall, Cheshire, and Leeswood Hall in Flintshire.

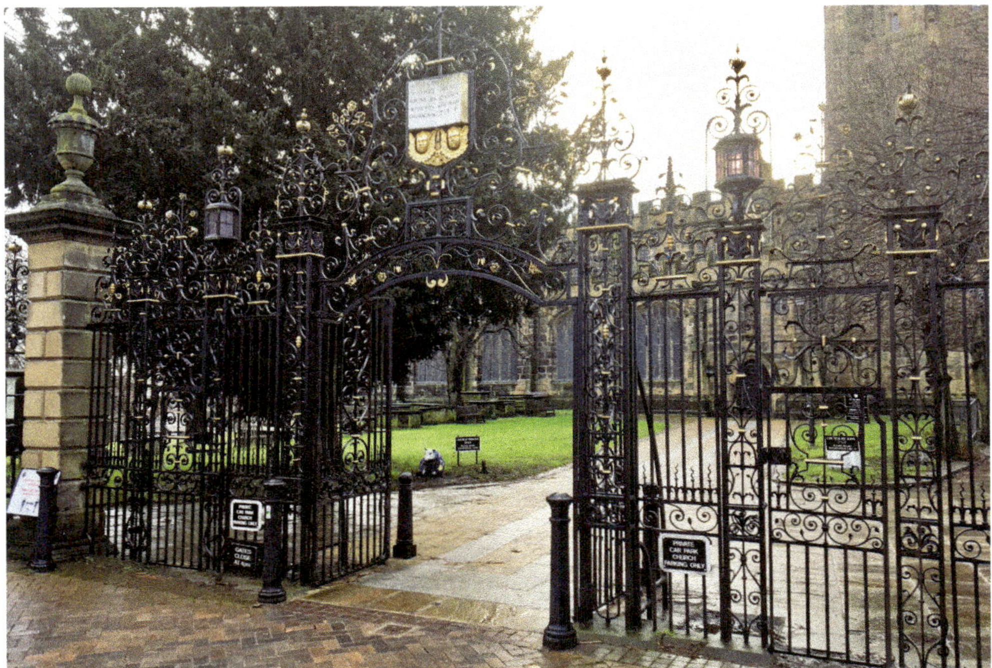

St Giles' Church gates, by Robert Davies, date from 1720. The chancel gates and choir rail have been attributed to his father, Hugh Davies, and date from the late seventeenth century.

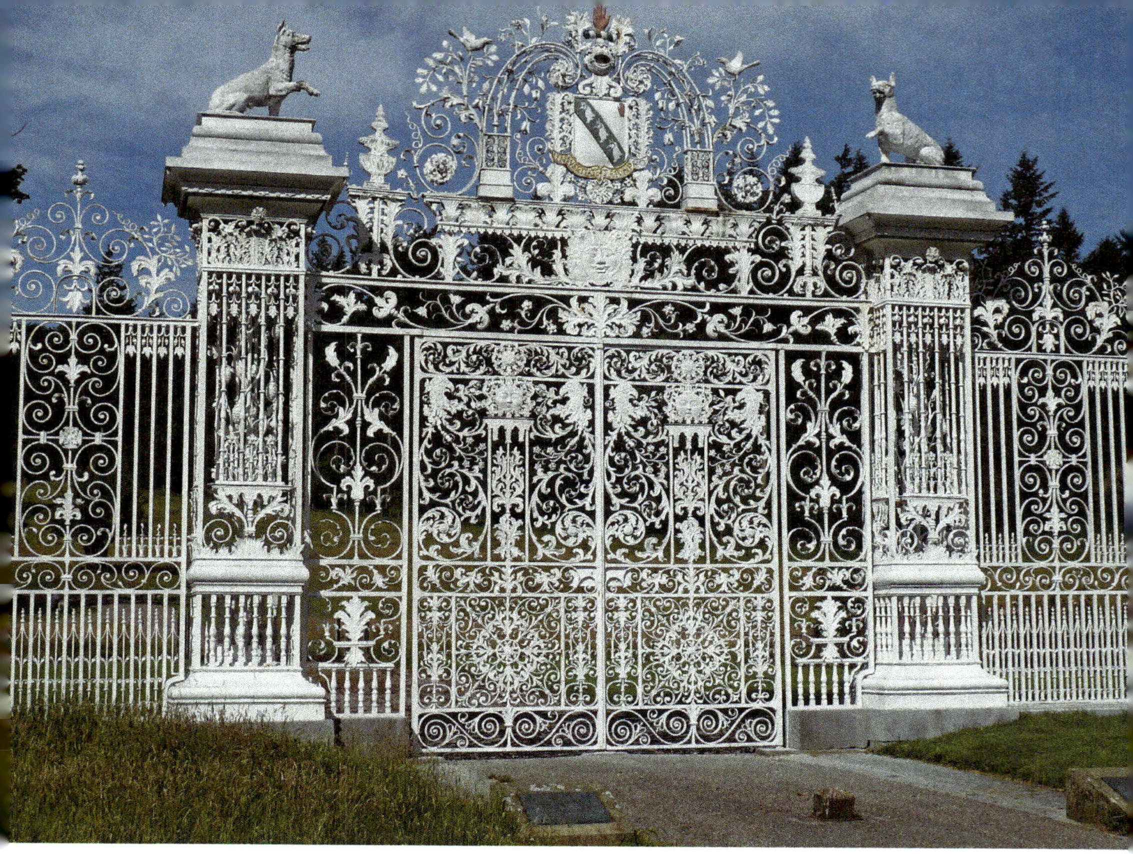

Above: Chirk Castle gates, made by the Davies brothers between 1712 and 1719. They originally stood at the north front of the castle, and were moved to the New Hall entrance in 1770. They were moved to their present position in 1888.

Below: Chirk Castle gates showing some of the detail.

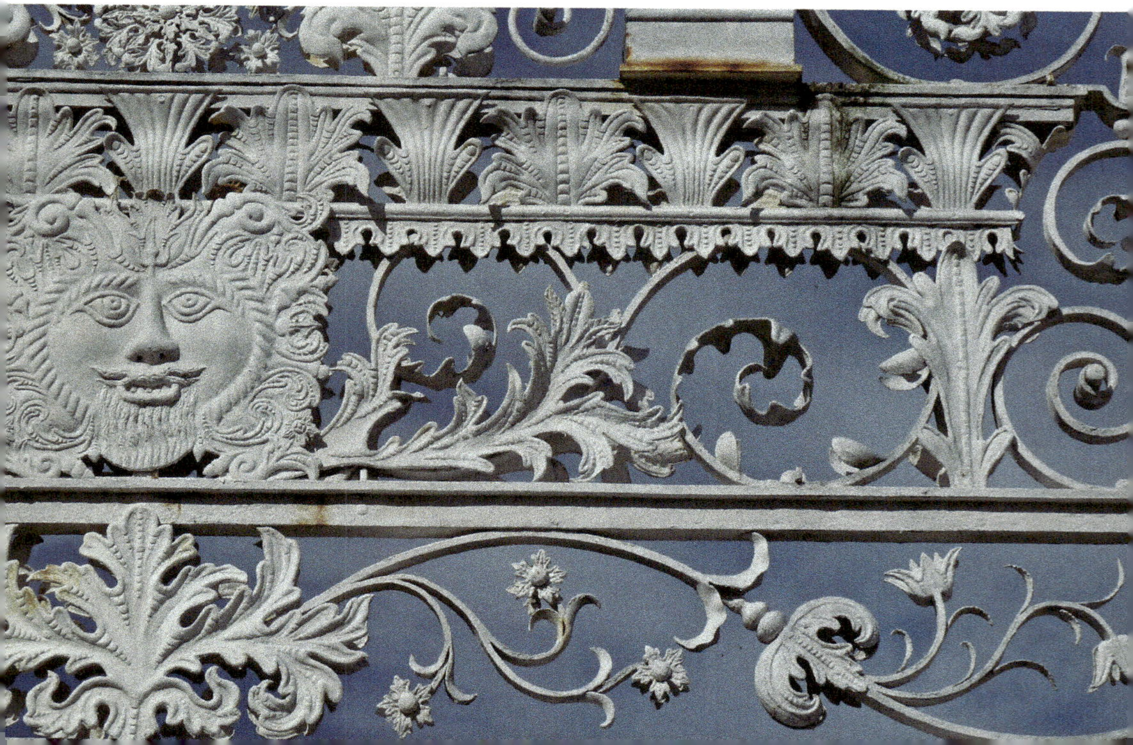

Dissenters Burial Ground, Rhosddu

It is thought that this burial ground was laid out by the Independents in the 1650s during the Interregnum. One of the first to be buried here was the theologian and writer Morgan Llwyd, who died in 1659. During the eighteenth century, the burial ground was being used and maintained by the Chester Street Baptist Church. At the entrance to the burial ground is a monument to Morgan Llwyd, which was unveiled by Mrs Margaret Lloyd George in April 1912. In 1960, the burial ground came under the care of Wrexham Borough Council, and the headstones were moved and the ground cleared. It was reopened as the Morgan Llwyd Memorial Park in 1963.

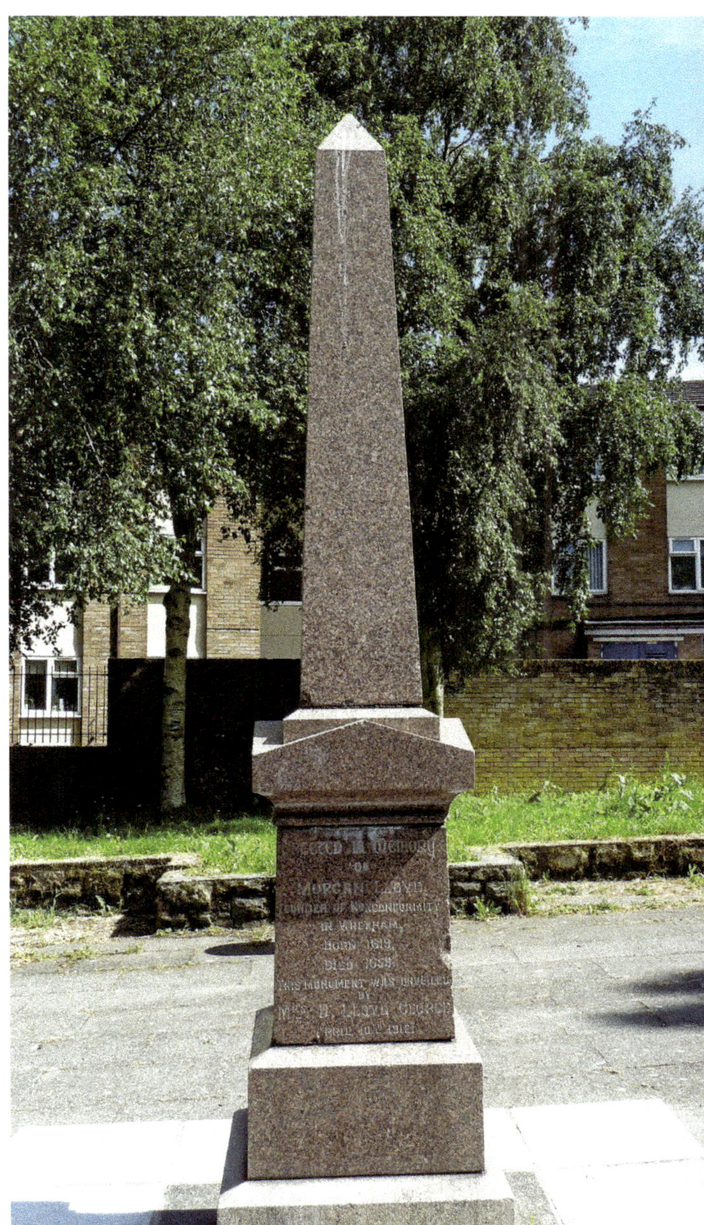

Dissenters Burial Ground, Rhosddu. Now laid out as a park, with many of the gravestones placed against the walls. This memorial to Morgan Llwyd stands at the entrance to the burial ground.

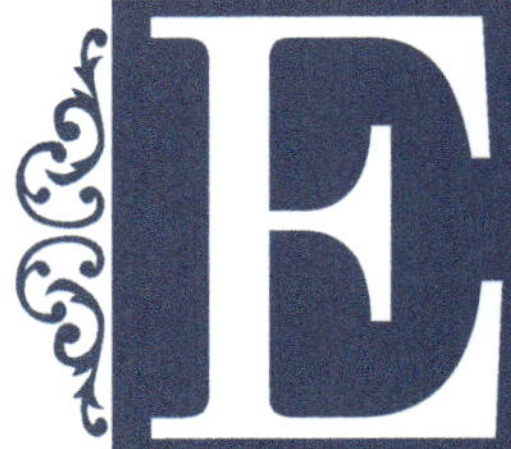

Eagles Meadow

The concrete and brick monolith that is now Eagles Meadow Shopping Centre belies the importance of this area in Wrexham's history. Eagles Meadow is so named because it was the grassed area behind the Eagles Hotel, which was the former name of the Wynnstay Arms. Although the area was subject to flooding from the River Gwenfro, there was a bowling green at the western end of the meadow. From 1874, quarterly horse sales were held here. What appears to have started as a fairly small operation quickly grew, and by 1891 stabling for 350 horses had been built together with sale rings and a quarter mile long trotting track. Reportedly, the sales attracted buyers and sellers from all over Britain, Ireland and Europe.

Eagles Meadow has had many uses over the years. The present shopping centre was opened amid some controversy in October 2008. At the time the centre opened there were some sixty-three shops together with a number of high-rise apartments on the western edge of the site.

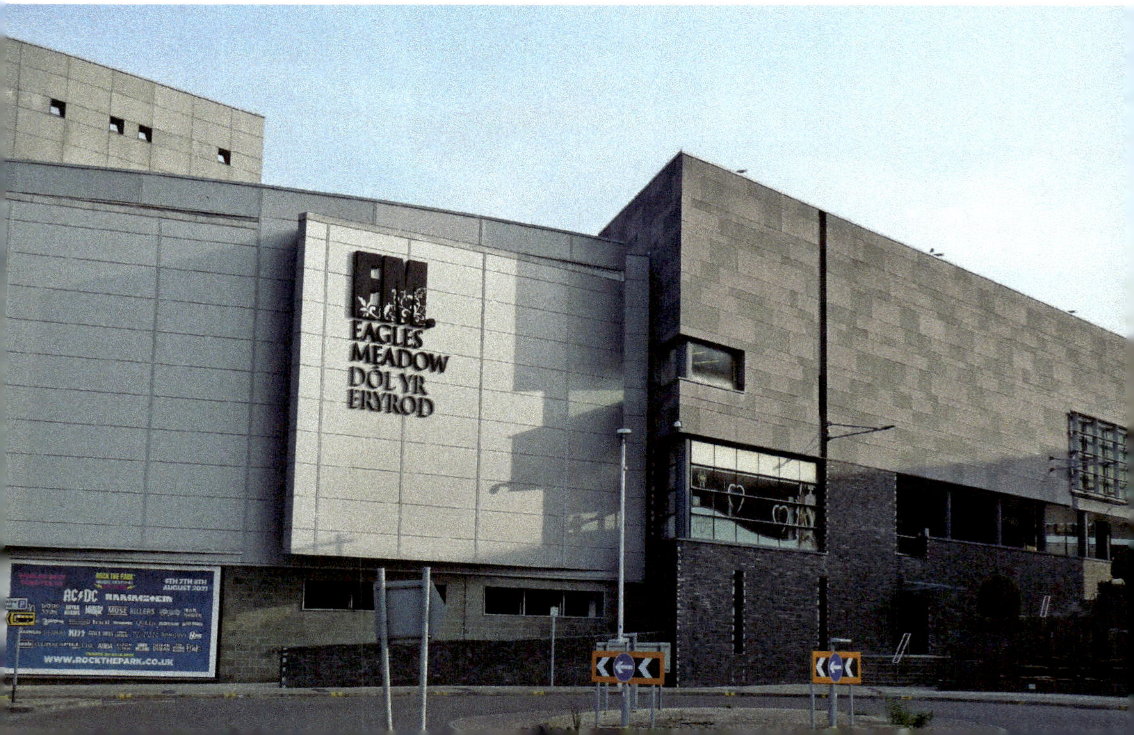

Although the sales lasted into the twentieth century, the decline in the need for horses eventually saw the end of horse sales on this scale. During the Second World War, Nissen huts were erected on Eagles Meadow to accommodate American servicemen. In the early 1970s, the land was divided between a car park and a small retail development. Maps from the early 1970s show a horse repository on the car park site. The car park then became the site for the main weekly market, which was moved from the old Beast Market.

The Eagles Meadow Shopping Centre was opened in October 2008 and boasts some 306,000 square feet of retail shopping space.

Erddig Hall

Erddig Hall stands 2 miles to the south of Wrexham. It was built between 1684 and 1687 for Josiah Edisbury, the High Sheriff of Denbighshire. The hall was designed by Thomas Webb, a master mason of Middlewich. The hall was sold to the master of the Chancery, John Meller, in 1714; he refurbished and enlarged the house, adding two wings in the 1720s. Meller died in 1733 and the house passed to his nephew Simon Yorke. The house remained in the Yorke family until 1973, when the last squire Philip Scott Yorke gave it to the National Trust. Several years earlier, a shaft from Bersham Colliery collapsed under the house, causing it to subside by 1.5 metres, affecting the structural integrity of the house to the extent that, without suitable underpinning it would, in all probability, have collapsed. It was strengthened using £120,000 compensation from the National Coal Board and the sales of parkland (£995,000 of which paid for the restoration of the house). The restoration was completed in 1977 and on 27 June HRH Prince Charles officially opened Erddig to the public. Erddig's walled garden is an important example of an eighteenth-century formal garden.

Erdigg Hall, built between 1684 and 1687 by Sir Josiah Edisbury, has been described as 'The jewel in the crown of Welsh country houses'.

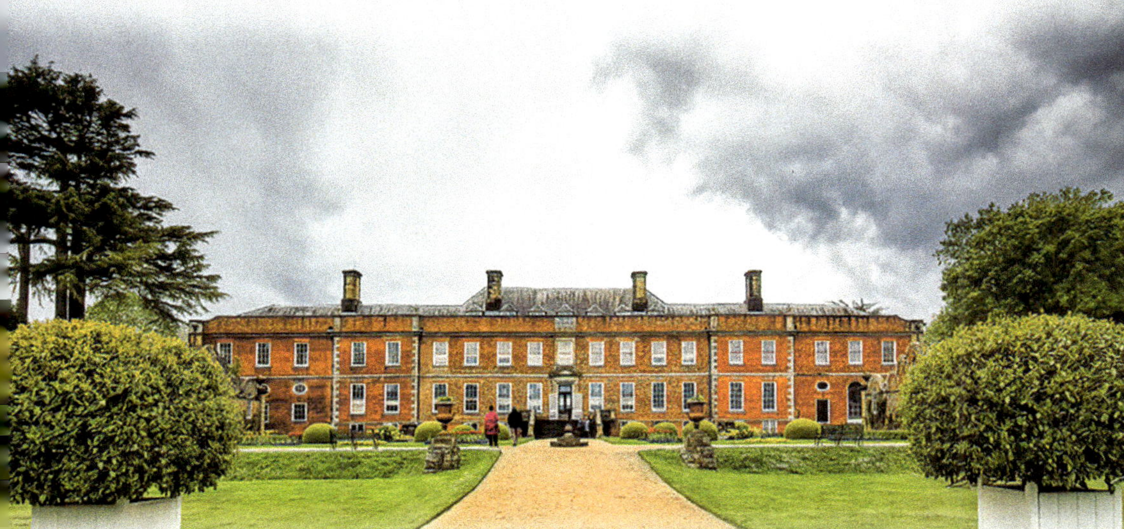

Exchange Station

Wrexham Exchange railway station was built by the Wrexham, Mold & Connah's Quay Railway in August 1865, although it was not opened to railway traffic until early in 1866. The station was sited alongside Wrexham General station, and the two linked by a footbridge. In November 1887, the line was extended into Wrexham terminating at Wrexham Central station and the original station was renamed Exchange station. In 1897, the Wrexham, Mold & Connah's Quay Railway went into receivership and was eventually taken over by the Great Central Railway in 1905. The Great Central itself became part of the LNER under the grouping of 1923. The original platform of the WM&CQ Railway became platform 4 of Wrexham General.

Fairs

Fairs in Wrexham were held on 12 March, 5 June and 8 September. However, after the change to the Gregorian calendar in 1752, these were changed to 23 March, 16 June and 19 September. In 1818, it was decided that in addition to fairs held on these dates there would also be fairs on 7 August and 29 October. There was also to be a new market day on the third Thursday of January specifically for horses, cattle, sheep and pigs. It is interesting that there is no fair in November. An Act of Parliament in 1677 endorsed the yearly bonds made at that time. Contracts between farmers and their workers expired on Old Martinmas Day (23 November), the end of the farming year. It is possible therefore that the October fair was also a hiring (statute) fair in addition to the merchandise being sold.

Fairs had generally died out by the late nineteenth century, with the development of indoor markets. Some specialised fairs persisted into the twentieth century, such as the horse fair in Wrexham. Today, the last vestige of fairs that started in the medieval period is the occasional pleasure fair that appears in the car park of WaterWorld.

Falklands Memorial

Near the Royal Welsh Fusiliers memorial at Bodhyfryd is a memorial to those members of the 1st Battalion of the Welsh Guards killed in the Falkland Islands in 1983.

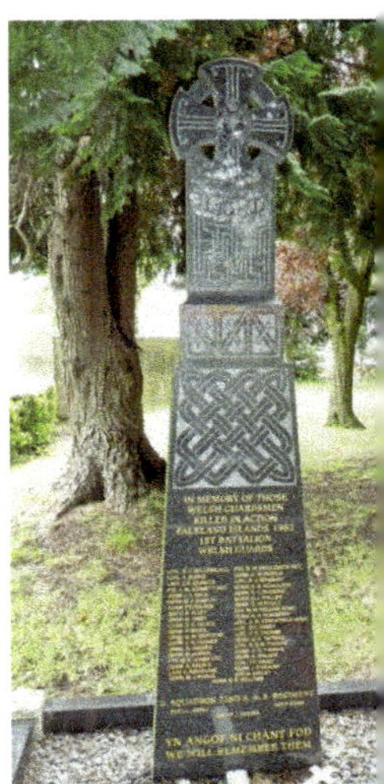

Falklands Memorial. This memorial to those Welsh guardsmen who died in the Falklands War stands in Bodhyfryd.

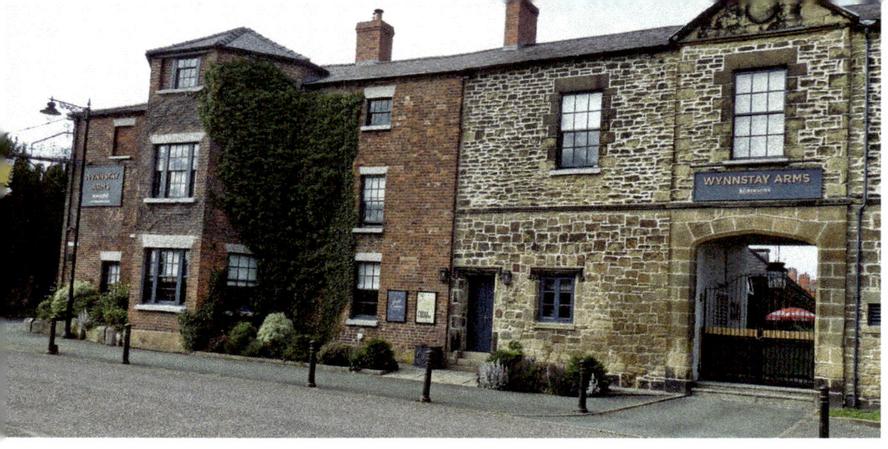

The Wynnstay Arms, Ruabon. It was here that the committee met to formalise the Welsh Football Association.

Football Association of Wales

The Football Association of Wales was founded at a meeting held at the Wynnstay Arms, Wrexham, on 2 February 1876. In May 1876, a further meeting was held, this time at the Wynnstay Arms, Ruabon, at which the title of the association was agreed and the constitution drawn up. This second meeting went on for so long that the local police constable came in and pointed out that it was past 'time' and the meeting would need to close. At this, Sir Watkin Williams-Wynn, who was attending the meeting, used his position as the local JP and sitting MP to go next door, open the court and extend the hotel's licensing hours, enabling the meeting to continue. The Football Association of Wales is the third oldest national association in the world.

Football

Wrexham Football Club was formed in 1864 by members of the Wrexham Cricket Club. It is the third oldest professional football club in the world and, arguably, the oldest football club in Wales. Whether or not you believe it to be the oldest club in Wales very much depends on which terrace you are standing on, since the same claim is also made by Newtown Football Club. There is no doubting the Wrexham club's original formation date, and they played their first match in October 1864. However, crowd trouble led to the club being expelled from the FA in 1883 and being reformed in 1884 as Wrexham Olympic. The Olympic name was dropped in 1888. In 2021, Wrexham FC embarked on a new stage of its history when Hollywood actors Ryan Reynolds and Rob McElhenny became the new owners following a £2 million investment in the club. In April 2023, after fifteen years in the National League, Wrexham FC finally returned to the Football League. The Wrexham-Newtown debate was summarised by the *Powis County Times* in 2018, claiming that Newtown had been formed in 1875, and the Powis club claimed that the club reformed in Wrexham in 1883 was not the same club that had been formed in 1864.

The club's home ground is the Racecourse Ground on Mold Road, which is the world's oldest international stadium.

Given the part played by Wrexham in the development of football in the Principality, it is appropriate that Wales National Football Museum should be established in Wrexham Museum.

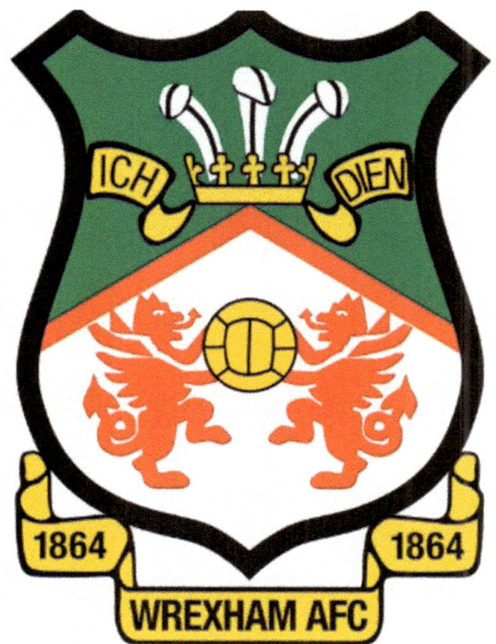

Right: The badge of Wrexham Football Club proudly displays its 1864 foundation date.

Below: Wrexham FC's Racecourse Ground, Mold Road, the world's oldest international stadium.

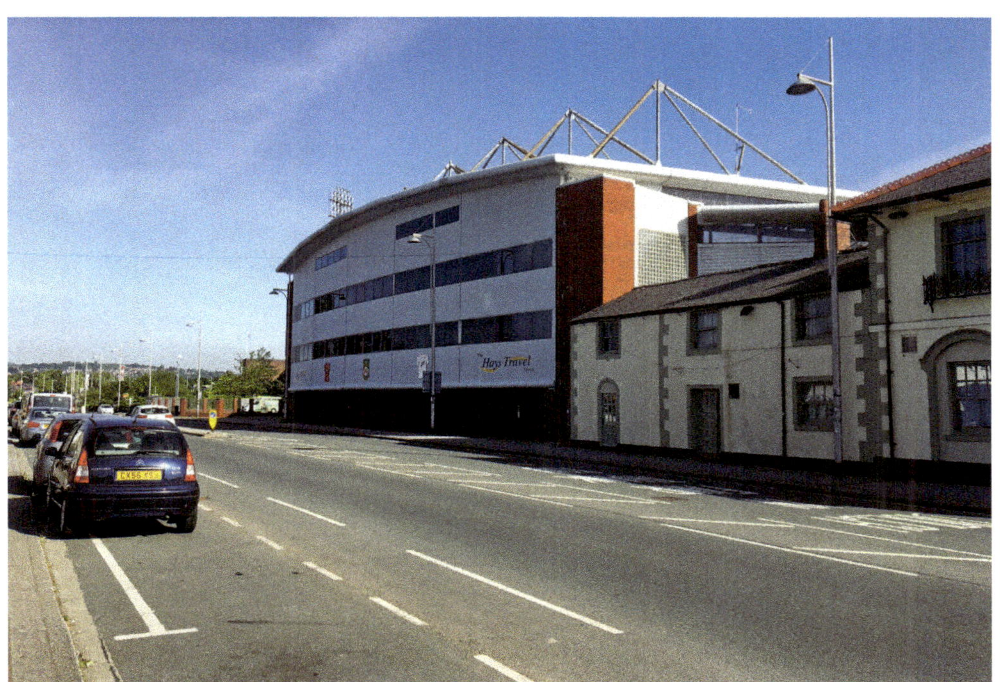

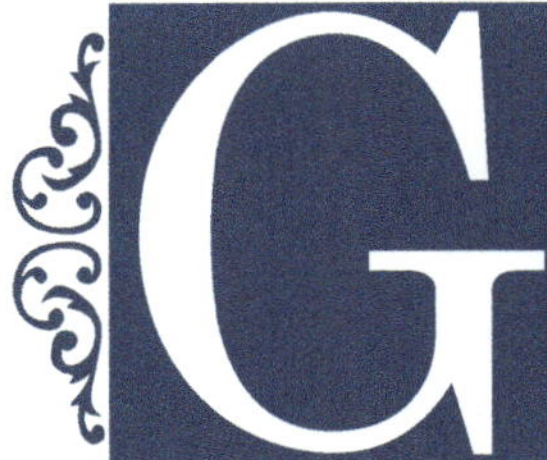

Garden Village

Garden villages were designed to be distinct self-contained communities of between 1,500 and 10,000 homes. They would have their own facilities such as shops, schools and churches. The plans for Wrexham Garden Village were drawn up by G. L. Sutcliffe in 1913 and were originally intended to cover a much wider area. Sutcliffe had been involved with several similar schemes and was very much influenced by the Arts and Crafts movement. He was responsible for the design and layout of the first 245 houses, which were completed by the end of 1914. Sutcliffe died in 1915 and was succeeded by T. Alwyn Lloyd of Cardiff and it was at this time that the plans were modified due to the practical and financial difficulties brought about by the First World War. It was unfortunate, therefore, that the planned village institute, shops and places of worship

A general view of Garden Village. Plans for the Garden Village were originally drawn up in 1913 and the first 254 houses completed by the end of 1914.

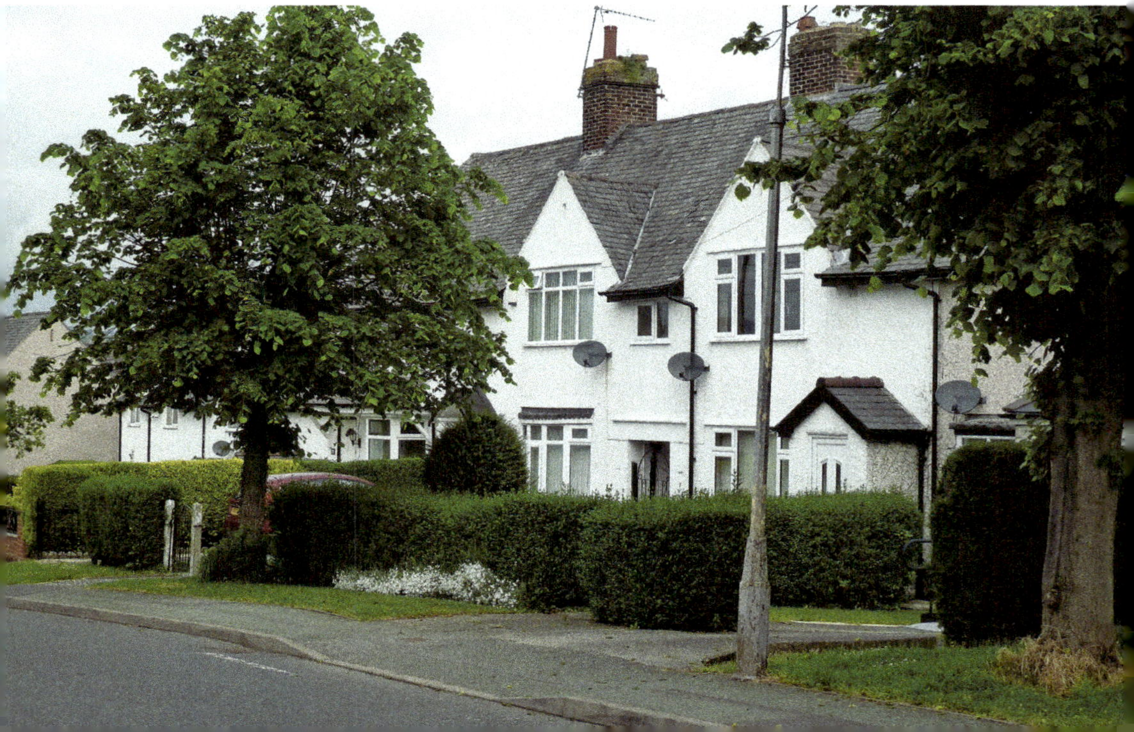

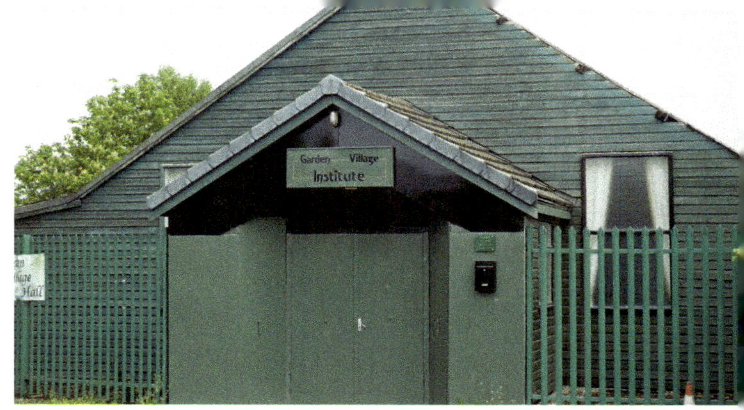

The Garden Village
Community Centre.

were never built. Although St Margaret's Church was built in 1928. The Garden Village was the inspiration for the Acton Park estate, which was started in 1921 and built on 60 acres of Acton Park purchased by the Borough Council. The houses on the new estate were designed by Sir Patrick Abercrombie, and there are many similarities between the two estates. Garden Village celebrated its centenary in 2013.

Guildhall

Following its incorporation as a borough in May 1857, Wrexham Council leased part of Bryn-y-Ffynnon House as a municipal building. In 1883, they purchased, as their Guildhall, the old Wrexham Grammar School building in Chester Street. Over the next half century or so, there were numerous proposals for a new Guildhall. However, it was not until 1951 that the council purchased the former vicarage and grounds of Llwyn Isaf as the site for a new Guildhall. Built in a neo-Georgian style, the new Guildhall was opened in May 1961 by HRH Princess Alexandra.

Wrexham Guildhall, Llwyn Isaf. Built to replace an earlier guildhall in Chester Street, the new building was opened in 1961 by HRH Princess Alexandra.

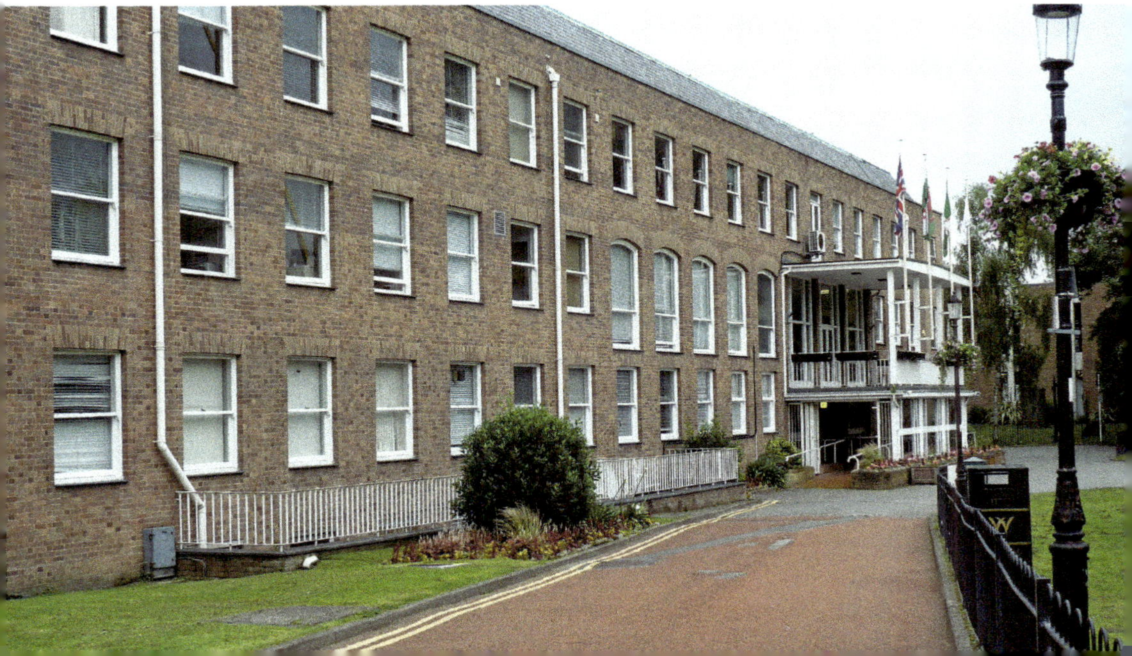

Gresford

The former coal mining village of Gresford lies just over 4 miles from Wrexham. In common with many border villages and towns it has gone through periods of English and Welsh dominance. In fact, at the time of the Domesday Book in 1086, it was recorded within the Cheshire Hundred of Duddestan. However, during the period 1170–1203, the whole area was resettled by Welsh aligned to Owain Gwynedd. From the early part of the twentieth century, the village was the site of one of the areas largest coal mines.

The late fifteenth-century All Saints Church, Gresford, has been described as the finest parish church in Wales; in fact, in designating it a Grade I building CADW had said that the church 'was an exceptional example of a late medieval church with fine medieval glass and furnishings'. Just why such a large and well-fitted church should have been built in so small a village is a matter a conjecture; it has been suggested however, that it may possibly have been a place of pilgrimage.

Gresford was also the scene of one of the country's worst mining disasters. The Westminster and United Collieries Group had begun to sink their two shafts in 1909 and completed them in 1911. The two shafts were the deepest in the Denbighshire coalfield at 2,264 and 2,252 feet, respectively. By 1934, some 2,200 miners were employed at the pit – 1,800 below ground and 350 on the surface. On 22 September 1934, an explosion and underground fire killed 266 miners. Despite numerous rescue attempts, only eleven bodies were ever recovered. The colliery closed in 1973.

St Mary's Church, Gresford, a splendid example of fifteenth-century church architecture.

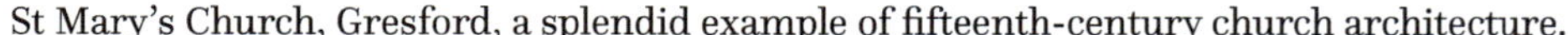

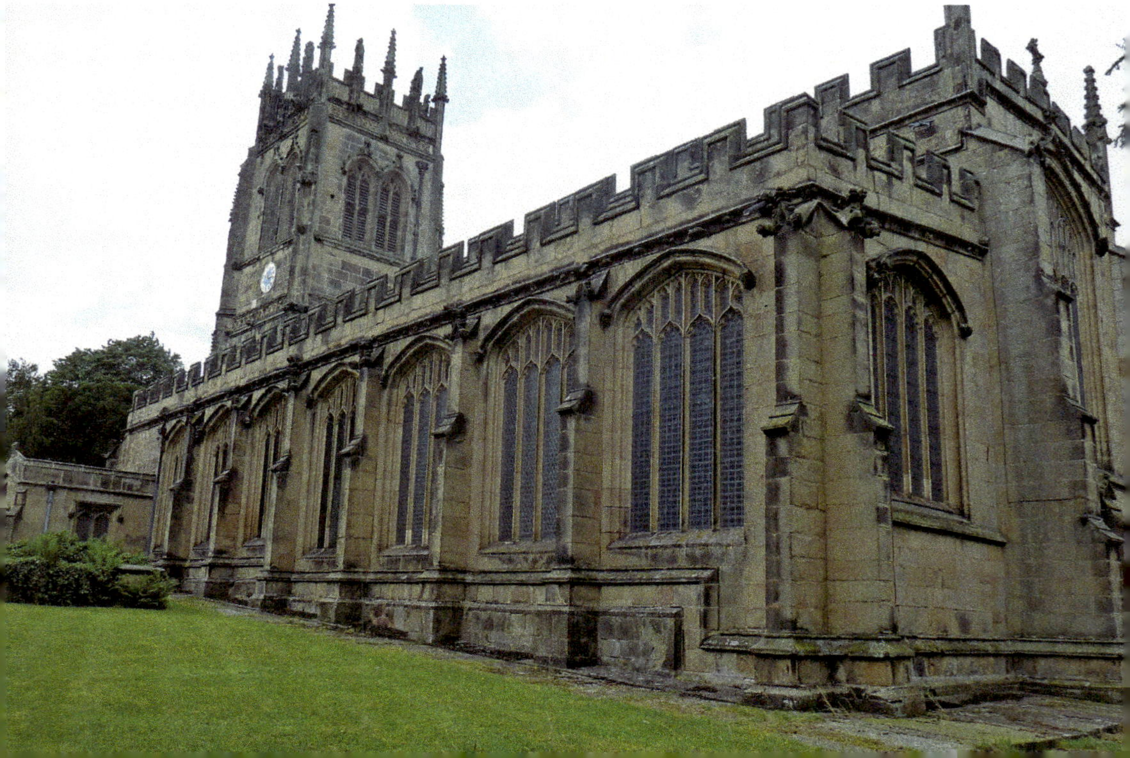

Gwyn, Richard

Richard Gwyn, who was also known by the Anglicised name Richard White, was born in Montgomeryshire in around 1537. Following studies at both Oxford and Cambridge he became a schoolmaster, first at Overton and then in Wrexham. He was an adherent to the 'old faith' and, for a time, he conformed to the new religion. Eventually, however, he was reconciled to the Catholic faith. Owing to his recusancy he was arrested and imprisoned on a number of occasions. He was offered his freedom if he would conform to the Anglican Church, but he steadfastly refused to do this. With two other recusants, he was indicted for high treason in October 1583 and was sentenced to be hanged, drawn and quartered. The sentence was carried out in Wrexham Beast Market on 15 October 1584. Richard Gwyn was canonised by Pope Paul VI in 1970 as one of the Forty Martyrs of England and Wales.

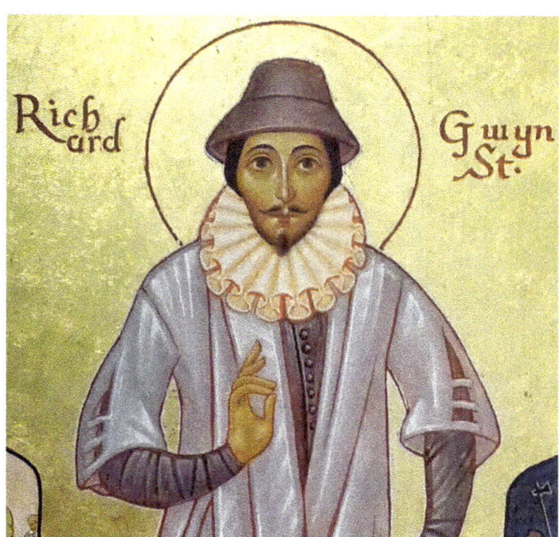

St Richard Gwyn was hanged, drawn and quartered in Wrexham Beast Market in 1584.

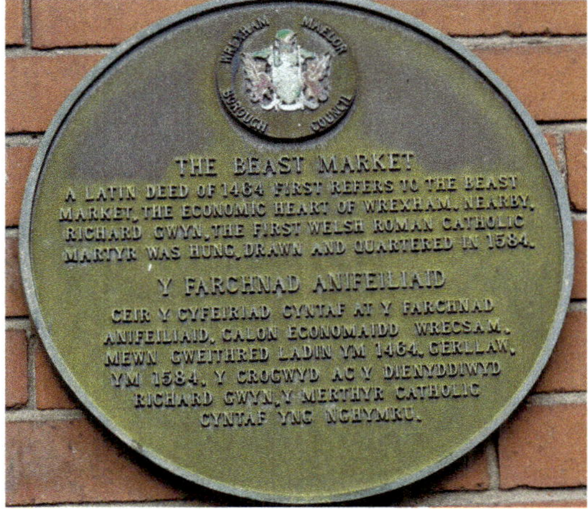

A plaque in the Beast Market recording the early (1484) date of the Beast Market and the hanging of Richard Gwyn.

Hightown Barracks

Built in a Gothic Revival style, Hightown Barracks date from 1877, when they were built to serve as the depot for the 23rd Brigade. In August 1877, the Royal Welsh Fusiliers (23rd Regiment of Foot) moved in, along with the Royal Denbighshire Militia. The RWF remained at Hightown until 1968, when their HQ was moved to Caernarfon. During both the First and Second World Wars, recruit training was carried out at the barracks. Although the barracks are still used by the military, part of the original barracks area has now been taken over by the Department of Transport as a driving test centre.

Hightown Barracks, for many years the regimental depot of the Royal Welch Fusiliers.

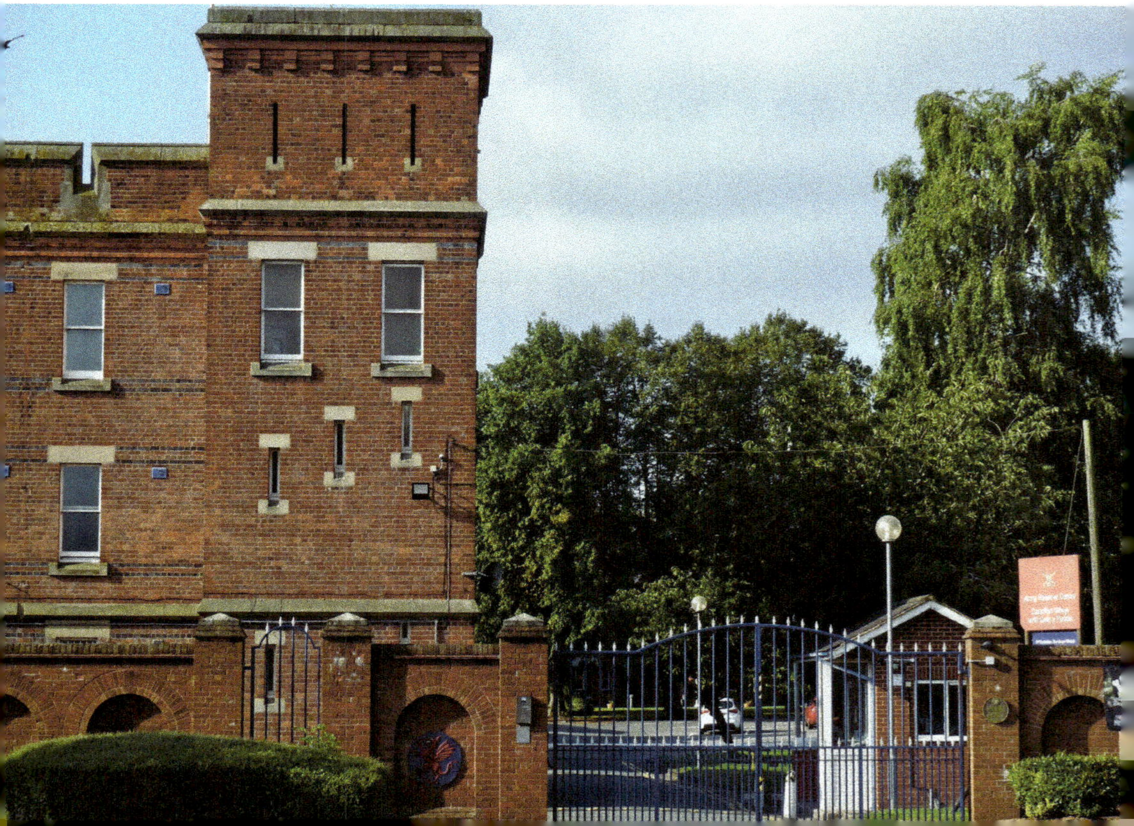

Hospitals

The Dispensary in Yorke Street was founded by Dr Thomas Taylor Griffith and Sir Watkin Williams Wynn. Opened in 1833, it was intended for the use of labourers and their families and servants earning less than £3 a year and for anyone else unable to pay for medical advice or medicines , proving they were not in receipt of poor relief.

With the population of Wrexham growing, there was a need for better healthcare provision in the town and, in 1836, a fund was established to pay for an infirmary. Fundraising in 1837 brought in £1,053, sufficient to start a new building on Mold Road. The building was designed by Edward Welch in a classical style and was completed by 1838. The first ward for in-patients was opened in 1840. Today, the building is part of Wrexham Glyndwr University.

Croesnewydd Hospital was originally built as a fever ward for the Wrexham Poor Law Union in 1912. Later, it was to be known as the Joint Fever Hospital. Following the abolition of Poor Law Unions in 1929, the hospital was extended to include new buildings for the elderly infirm. These new buildings, which were known as Plas

The Memorial Hospital, built to commemorate those who died in the First World War and opened in 1926. The hospital closed in 1986 and is now part of Coleg Cambria.

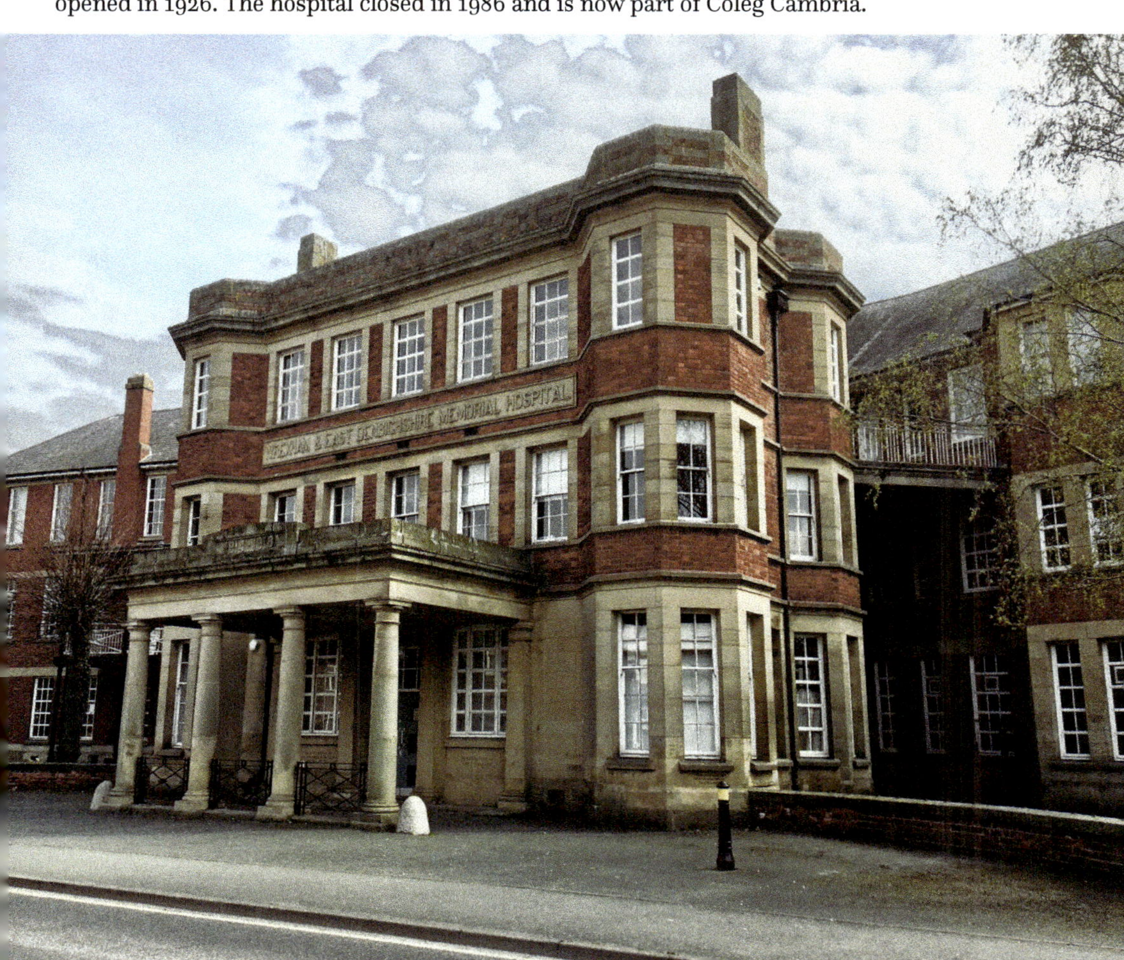

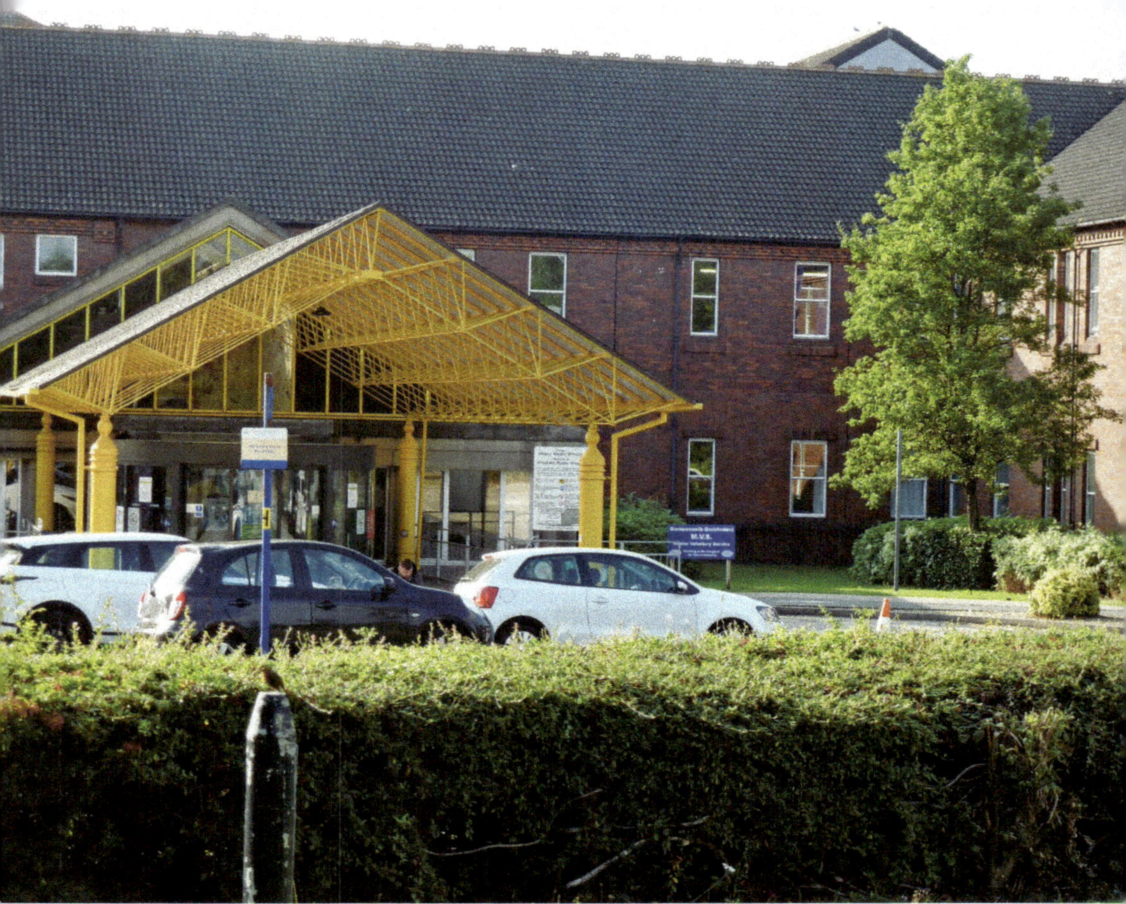

Wrexham Maelor Hospital. The first phase of this new hospital was opened in 1986, with the second phase being opened in 1998.

Maelor, were opened by David Lloyd George in 1934. The hospital was used as an emergency hospital in the Second World War, and became known as Wrexham Emergency Hospital.

The Wrexham and East Denbighshire War Memorial Hospital was built as a memorial to the men of Wrexham and East Denbighshire who were killed in the First World War, and would replace the old Wrexham Infirmary. The foundation stone was laid by HRH Edward Prince of Wales on 2 November 1923. The hospital was officially opened by HRH Prince Henry, Duke of Gloucester, on 9 June 1926. The hospital closed in 1986 to be replaced by the Maelor General Hospital.

With the advent of the National Health Service in 1948, the War Memorial Hospital, together with the other Wrexham hospitals, were grouped together and known as the Maelor General Hospital.

The first phase of the present Maelor General Hospital was opened in March 1985, and officially opened by HRH the Duchess of Kent on 26 October 1986. The services provided by the Wrexham and East Denbighshire War Memorial Hospital then transferred to the Maelor. The second phase was opened by HRH the Duke of Kent in July 1998. Today, Wrexham Maelor Hospital is the second largest hospital in Wales.

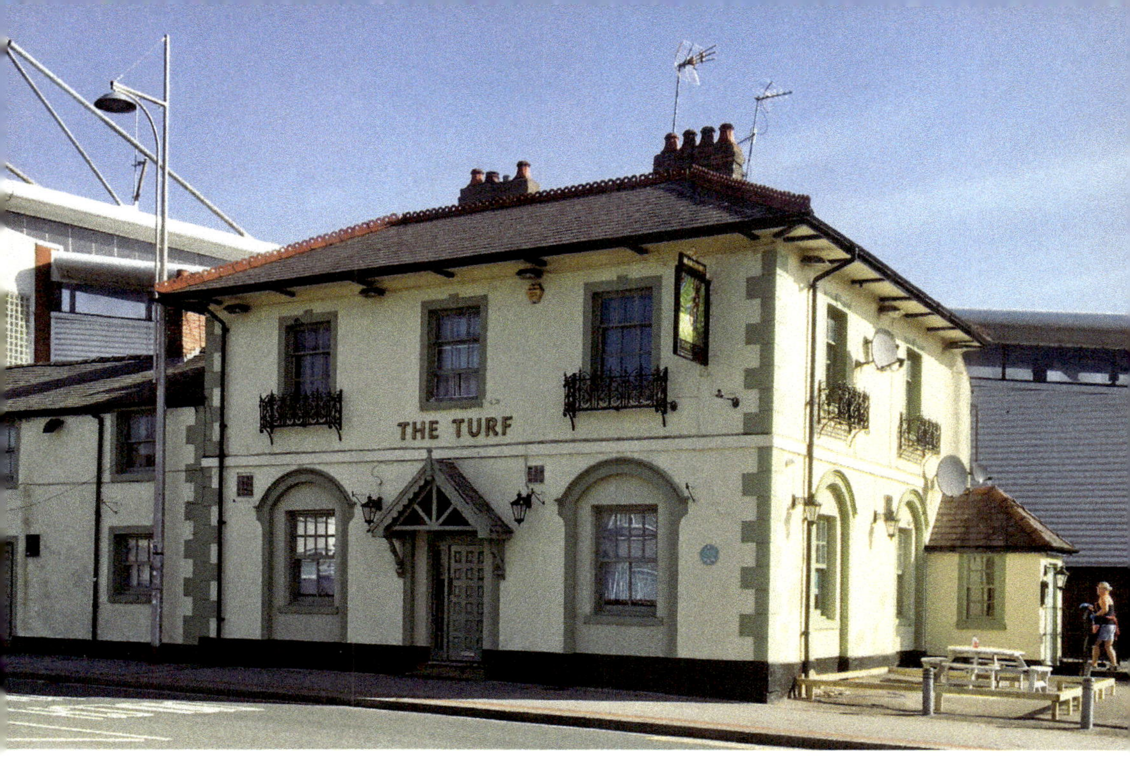

The Turf, standing adjacent to the football ground, is a reminder of the town's horse racing past.

Horse Racing

The only tangible reminders of Wrexham's involvement with horse racing is the Racecourse Football Ground and the Turf Inn. While today horse racing today is carried on at Bangor-on-Dee racecourse, in the nineteenth century it was part of the sporting scene in Wrexham. The races were instigated by Sir Watkin Williams Wynn and held on the course established on Mold Road. Initially, the races involved the Wrexham Yeomanry Cavalry, the first race being run in September 1807. The race meeting lasted some three days, and continued annually until 1825, when it was reduced to two days. Racing appears to have stopped in 1858, only to be revived again in 1867 as the Wrexham Autumn Sports. This became the Wrexham Races in 1872. In 1876, Sir Watkin granted the use of the racecourse to the local militia, which rather put paid to any form of racing. However, for about ten years from 1890, pony racing was held on the course.

Horseshoe Falls

Much to the disappointment of many visitors, Horseshoe Falls is not a cascading waterfall, but a weir on the River Dee about 3 miles north-west of Llangollen. The distinctive shaped weir, which is 140 metres long, enables water to be pumped from the River Dee to the Llangollen Canal. William Jessop proposed this site on the River

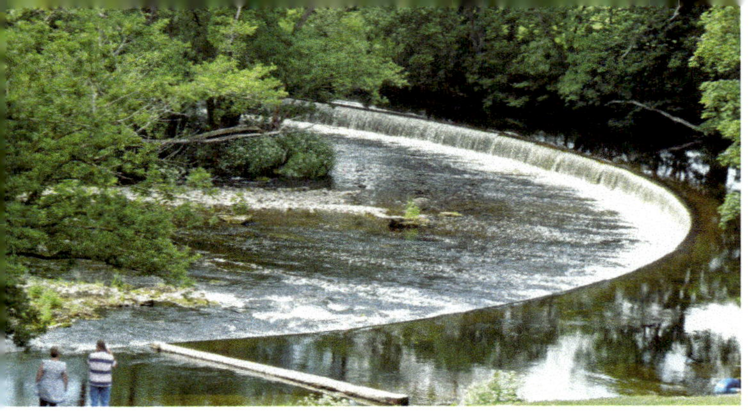

Horseshoe Falls. William Jessop proposed this site on the River Dee as a water source for the canal as early as 1795. The 460-foot-long weir was designed by Thomas Telford and was in operation by 1808.

Dee as a water source and it was designed by Thomas Telford. The weir is only 1.22 metres high, which makes it less susceptible to flood damage. It is built of stone with a capping of bull-nosed cast iron. The use of iron, which was added in 1822, was something of an innovation at the time.

Holt Bridge

Holt Bridge is considered one of the most important late medieval bridges in Wales. Spanning the River Dee between Holt and Farndon, it crosses the border between Wales and England. The date of the original bridge is unknown, although an earlier bridge is mentioned in a trial of 1368. The present bridge is thought to be fifteenth or sixteenth century. It is built of local red sandstone and has eight segmental arches with eight cutwaters and recesses. The bridge figured prominently in the Civil Wars of the seventeenth century, with both sides trying to take control of the crossing. The bridge was taken for Parliament by William Brereton and Thomas Myddleton on 9 November 1643.

Holt Bridge. The bridge spans the Welsh-English border and was captured for Parliament by William Brereton and Thomas Myddleton in 1643.

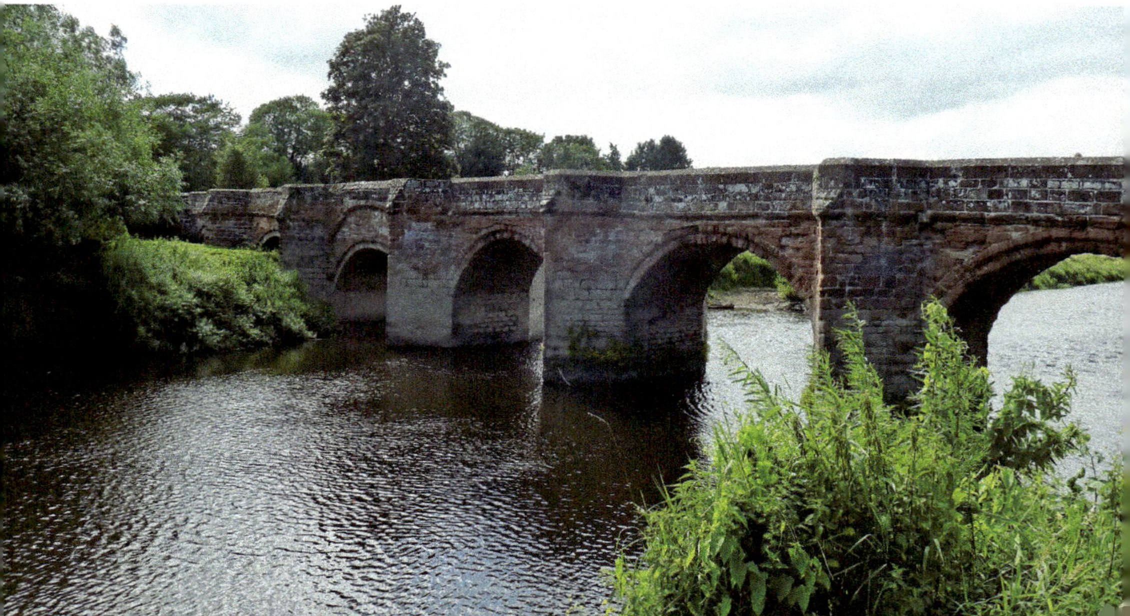

Infirmary

In 1836, a fund was set up to pay for an infirmary to replace the Dispensary in York Street. Sufficient money was available for work to begin on a new building on Mold Road in 1837. This was a sandstone building in a classical style designed by Edward Welch and was completed by 1838. The first ward for in-patients was opened in 1840. As with most hospitals in pre-NHS days, it was operated on a subscription basis. Subscribers paying 1 guinea or donating 10 guineas were entitled to become governors and could recommend up to twelve persons each year for treatment, inclusive of one

The infirmary, Mold Road. Opened in 1840, it served as Wrexham's hospital until 1926. It is now part of Wrexham Glyndwr University.

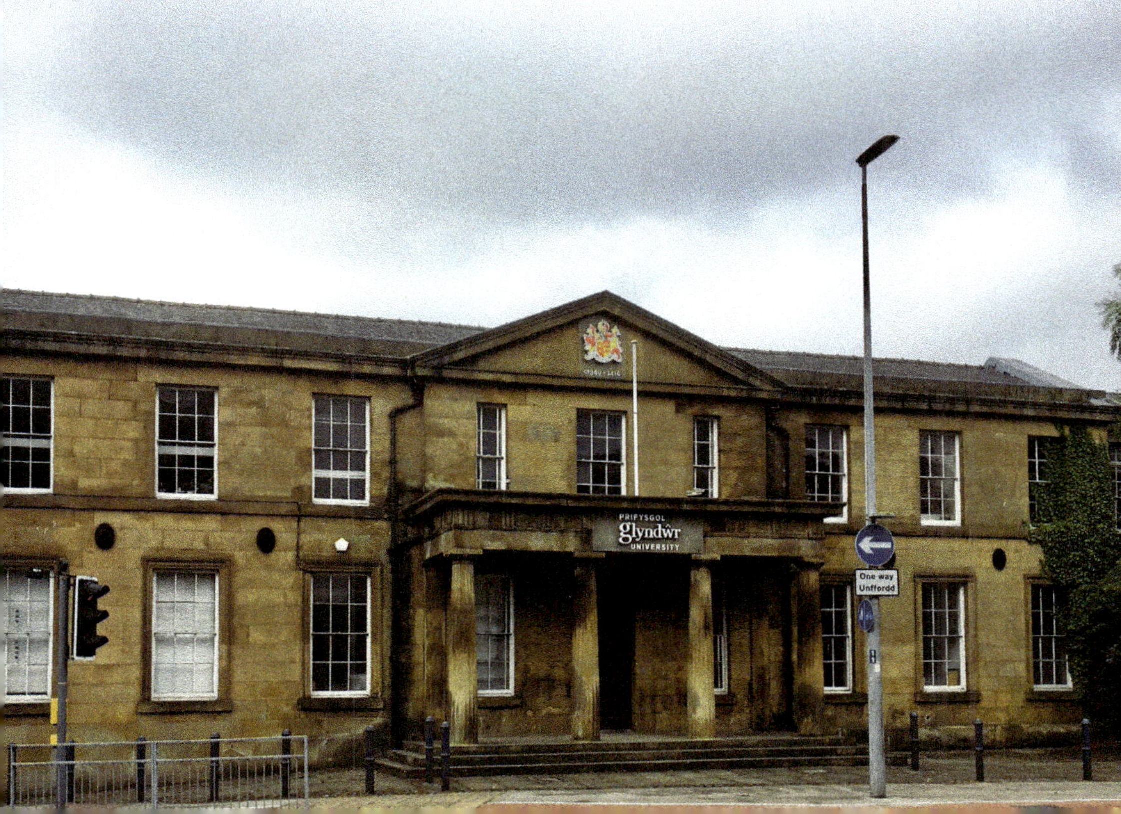

in-patient for whom an additional 10*s* 6*d* would have to be paid. Doctors visited the hospital on three days each week, although there was a full-time house surgeon. In-patients were required to provide their own bed linen and medicine bottles and all bandages had to be returned for reuse!

By 1860, the infirmary was dealing with over 2,000 patients each year, and in the twenty years since opening had dealt with over 40,000 patients. The Infirmary served as Wrexham's hospital until 1926, when the Wrexham and East Denbighshire War Memorial Hospital was opened.

The original infirmary on Mold Road was taken over by Denbighshire Technical College until the opening of the Plas Coch campus in 1953. The infirmary then became the Wrexham School of Art.

Island Green

This area of Wrexham may originally have been called Ireland Green; by 1833 there was a house on the bank of the Gwenfro called Island Green House. The area of the present shopping precinct was largely occupied by Wrexhan Central railway station, Hugh Price & Co. leather works and the Island Green Brewery. The area was redeveloped in the 1990s to create the shopping precinct and a new, much smaller, Central railway station, which was moved further to the west.

Island Green Shopping Centre. This area of Wrexham was largely occupied by the Central railway station, Hugh Price leather works and Island Green Brewery. The area was redeveloped in the 1990s.

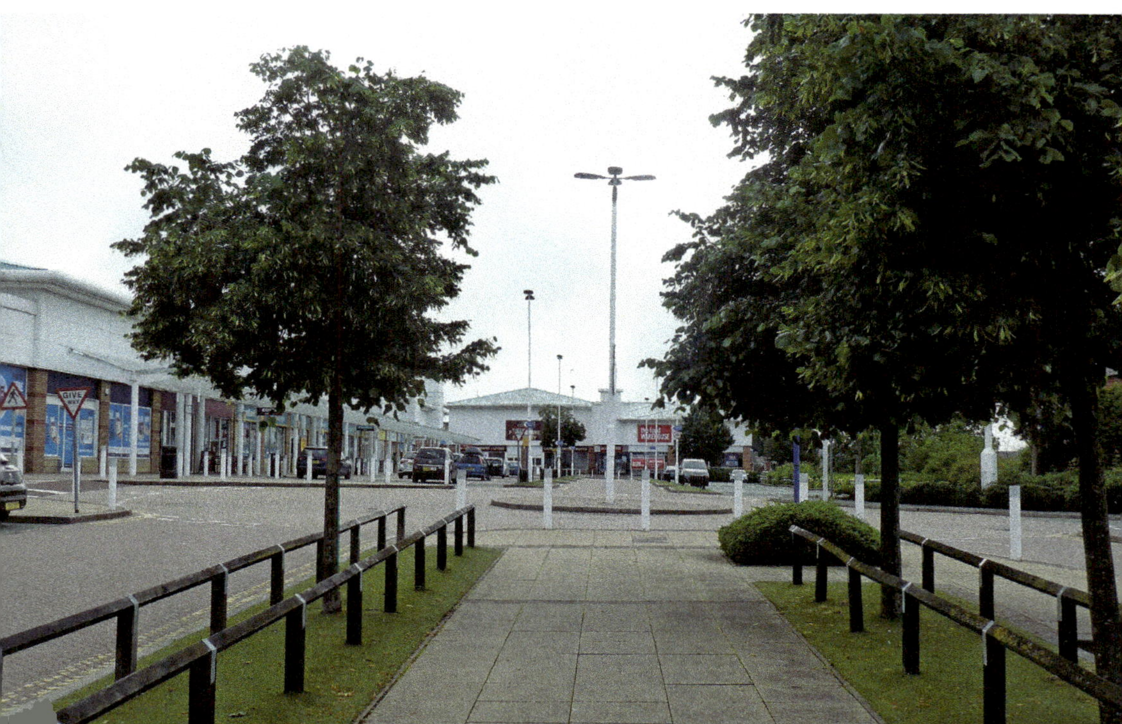

Island Green and Other Breweries

In the nineteenth century, there were nineteen commercial breweries operating in Wrexham and the history of brewing in the town might well be an object lesson in takeovers and mergers. Island Green Brewery was founded in 1856 by William and John Jones. The business continued successfully until the death of William Jones in 1904, when it was sold to Francis Huntley and George Mowat. Under their management the brewery continued to expand its outlets and by 1923 they had a total of seventy-three tied and leased pubs in the area. In 1931, the business merged with F. W. Soames and Dorsett Owen to form Border Breweries. The new company traded successfully for the next fifty years until it was taken over by Marston Brewery in 1984. Marston's itself was taken over by Wolverhampton and Dudley Breweries in 1998. Brewery Place is now the only reminder of the brewery that once stood on the Island Green site.

In 1881, a group of businessmen established the Wrexham Lager Beer Company, with a specialist brewery on Central Road. It would appear that the reason for establishing the brewery in Wrexham was because the quality of the Pant y Golfen spring in Maesgwyn was very similar to the water in Pilsen. The brewery began production in 1883 but, due to insufficient sales, it went into liquidation in 1892. However, the company was saved by its chairman Robert Graesser, who cleared its debts and enabled it to continue trading. In 1949, the company was bought by Ind Coope and Allsopp, who considerably expanded the brewery. In 1961, Ind Coope merged with Ansells and Tetley. Despite a modernisation programme and reviving the name Wrexham Lager Beer Company, the brewery closed on April 2000.

Island Green Brewery. Founded in 1856 by William & John Jones, it was sold in 1904 on the death of William Jones. Brewing continued on the site until well into the twentieth century.

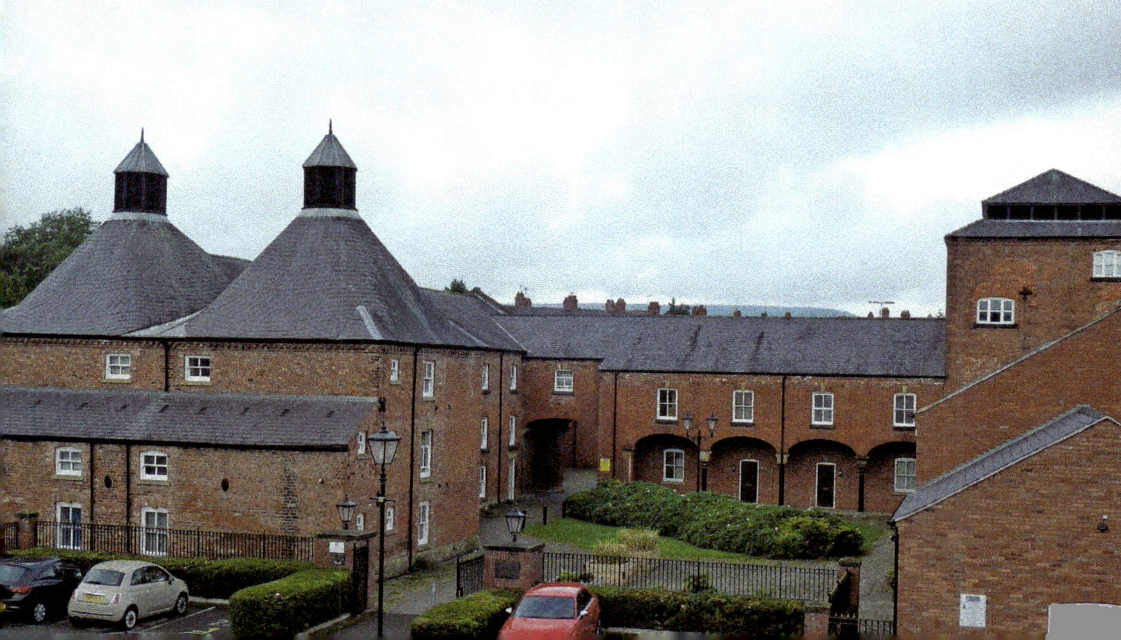

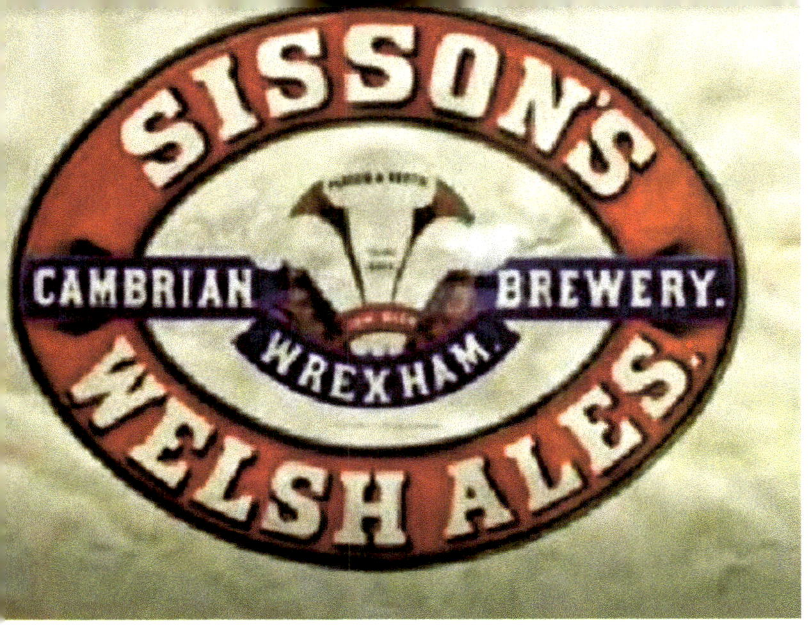

An advertisement for the Cambrian Brewery.

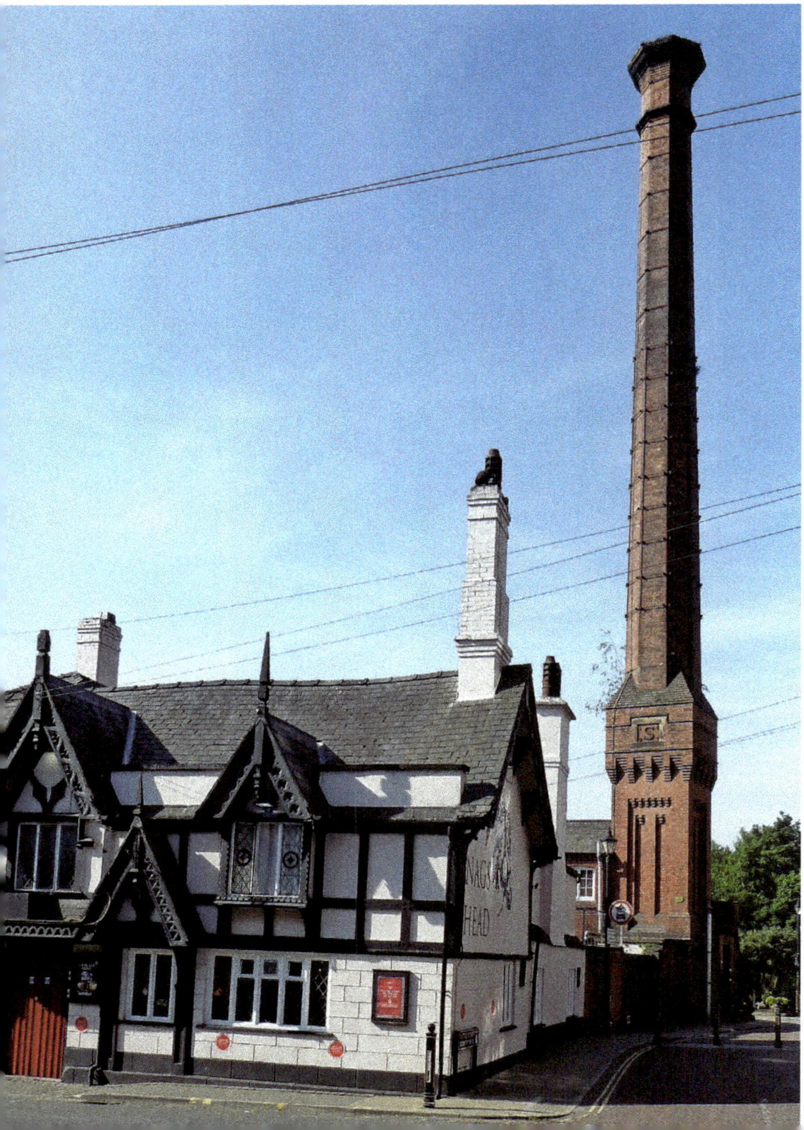

The Nags Head and the chimney of Soames Brewery. The brewery chimney, which was erected in 1894, stands at 130 feet and is Grade II listed.

Judge Jeffreys

Of the many well-known people born in Wrexham, George Jeffreys must surely be the most infamous. The sixth son of John and Margaret Jeffreys, George was born at Acton Hall on 15 May 1645. Following education at Shrewsbury and London, he became an undergraduate at Trinity College, Cambridge, but left after a year. He was admitted a member of the Inner Temple in 1663 and was called to the Bar in 1668. His rise in his profession was rapid. He was knighted in 1677 and became Recorder of London in 1678. He was active in the Popish Plot prosecutions and became Chief Justice of Chester in 1680 and Chief Justice of the King's Bench and a Privy Councillor to James II in 1683. In 1685, he became Baron Wem and Lord Chancellor. George Jeffreys is best remembered for the assizes held in the West Country following the Duke of Monmouth's rebellion. On instructions from the King, he dealt with Monmouth's followers with considerable severity. Over 1,000 rebels were in prison but, in the event, only 144 were hanged with some 850 being transported to the West Indies. The assizes became known as the 'Bloody Assizes' and Jeffreys earned himself the nicknames Bloody Jeffreys and the Hanging Judge. In 1688, on the accession of William and Mary, Jeffreys was sent to the Tower of London for his own safety. He died there in 1689.

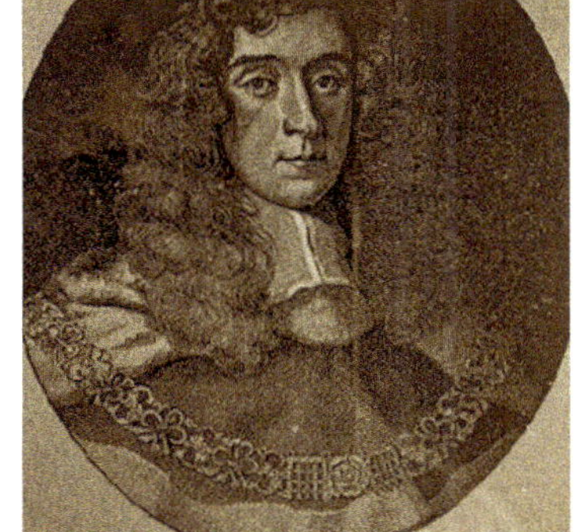

Judge Jeffreys. Born at Acton Hall in 1645, George Jeffreys earned his place in the history books and notoriety as a hanging judge following Monmouth's Rebellion in 1685.

Jessop, William (1745–1814)

Although Thomas Telford receives most of the kudos for the building of Pontcysyllte Aqueduct, none of Telford's ideas would have come to fruition without the support of William Jessop, who must surely be one of the unsung heroes of late Georgian and Victorian engineering. By the time of his appointment to the Ellesmere Canal in 1791, Jessop was already the dominant canal engineer in Britain. He had assisted John Smeaton with the construction of the Calder and Hebble & Aire and Calder navigations in Yorkshire. In 1772, Smeaton sent Jessop to Ireland to work on the Grand Canal of Ireland where he was working until 1787. In 1789, he was appointed Chief Engineer of the Cromford Canal in Derbyshire. By the time of the active end of his career in 1805, he had been involved in no less than fifteen canal projects, as well as harbours and railways. He was also well versed in the structural use of iron, having, with Benjamin Outram, been a founding partner in the Butterley Iron Works in Derbyshire. He was well known for his support of up-and-coming engineers. When Thomas Telford was appointed as Chief Engineer by the Ellesmere Canal Company, he had no previous experience in the design of canals. The advice and guidance given to him by William Jessop enabled him to make a success of the Poncysllte project. It is known that Jessop supported him even when the Ellesmere company thought that his designs were too ambitious.

Johnstown

The village of Johnstown forms part of the (former) mining community of Rhos. Before the development of Johnstown, the fields on either side of the Ruabon-Wrexham turnpike were owned by solicitor and Wrexham Alderman John Bury. The land was sold on the condition that the village would be named after Alderman Bury. The options were either Bury or John, hence Johnstown. The village seems to have developed in the early part of the nineteenth century as a ribbon development along the turnpike road. Some of the earlier brick-built houses in the village are built with brick from the Ponkey Brick and Tile Company (also known as the Aberderfyn Brickworks) while later buildings are constructed with brick from the Dennis brickworks.

Johnstown is actually built on part of Offa's Dyke and before the development of the village the area was known as Morton Wallicorum (i.e. Morton above the Dyke). The former Hafod colliery stood to the east of the village. Johnstown also became the terminus for the Wrexham trams. A horse-drawn tramway had been established between the New Inn at Johnstown and Wrexham toll bar in 1876. In 1900, the Wrexham and District Electric Tramway was formed by the British Electric Traction Group. The company established a depot on Maelor Road and re-laid and electrified the track between Johnstown and Wrexham, although by this time the toll bar had been removed and trams travelled right into the town centre. This tramway continued to operate until 1928, by which time competition from other forms of transport was beginning to make trams uneconomic.

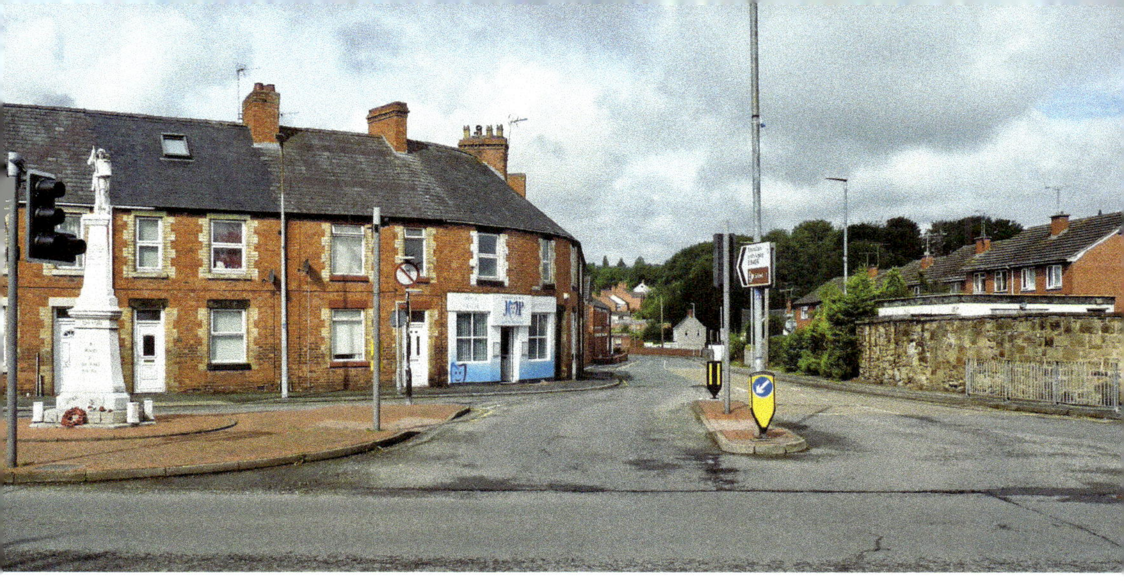

A general view of Johnstown, showing the war memorial and the road to Rhos.

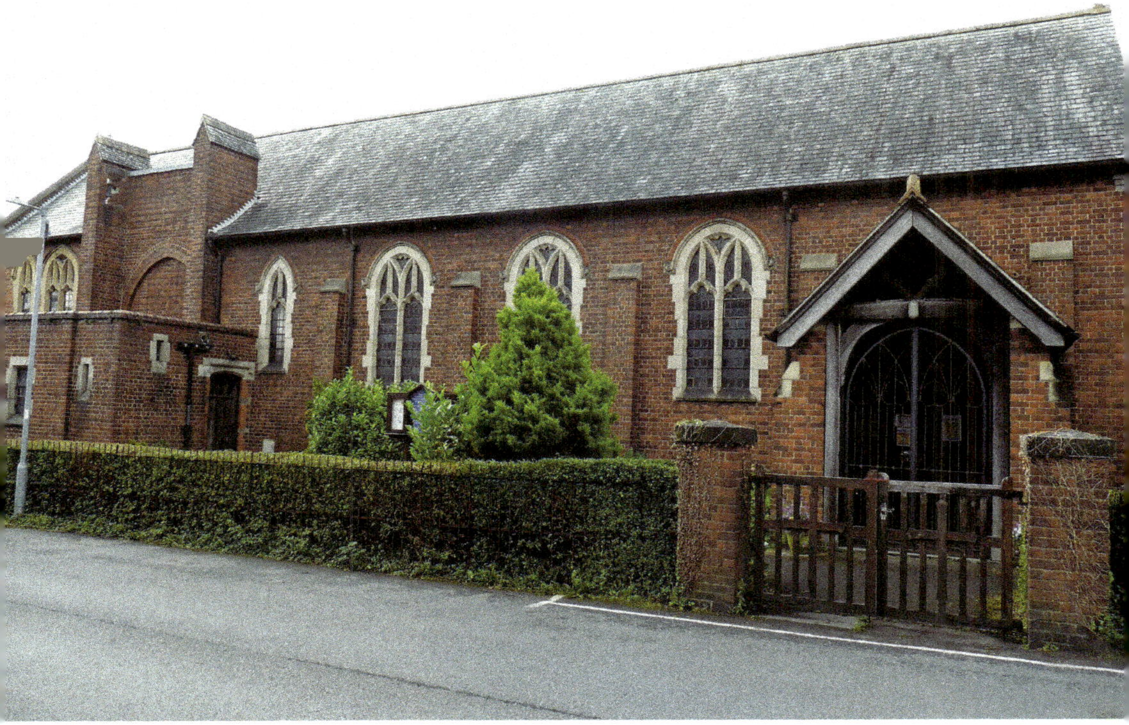

St Mary's Church, Johnstown, was built between 1926 and 1928 in a Perpendicular style to the design of E. Glyn Wooley. It was modified in 1957 with the completion of the chancel. It was built to replace an earlier iron church.

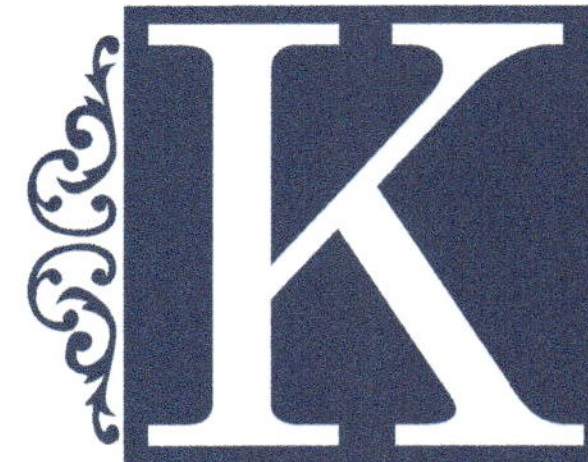

Kings Mills

During its lifetime, the building now known as Kings Mills has had a variety of names including New Mill, Lord's Mill, Queen's Mill, Prince's Mill and Crown Mill. This was the mill at which the people of Wrexham Regis had their flour ground. There has been a mill on this site since the fifteenth century and from 1495 until 1790, it was the property of the Crown. In 1790, the title to the mill was purchased by Philip Yorke.

Located on the bank of the river Clywedog, the present building is of three storeys in red sandstone. It is clearly an eighteenth-century building, but the date of the rebuilding is unclear, with both 1709 and 1769 being suggested.

The building remained in use as a mill until 1940 when it was closed. It remained empty for some years and, in the 1970s, its state was such that demolition was a very real possibility. However, it was renovated and, in July 1991, the mill was reopened as a visitor centre by HRH the Princess of Wales. The building has stood empty since 2013 and, in March 2021, Wrexham Council put it up for auction. However, it failed to reach its reserve price and remains empty. Covenant stating that the mill must be used as a public amenity has been in place since the property was acquired from the Erddig estate. Following a period of uncertainty, plans are now in hand to develop the building for a new use, which should secure its long-term future.

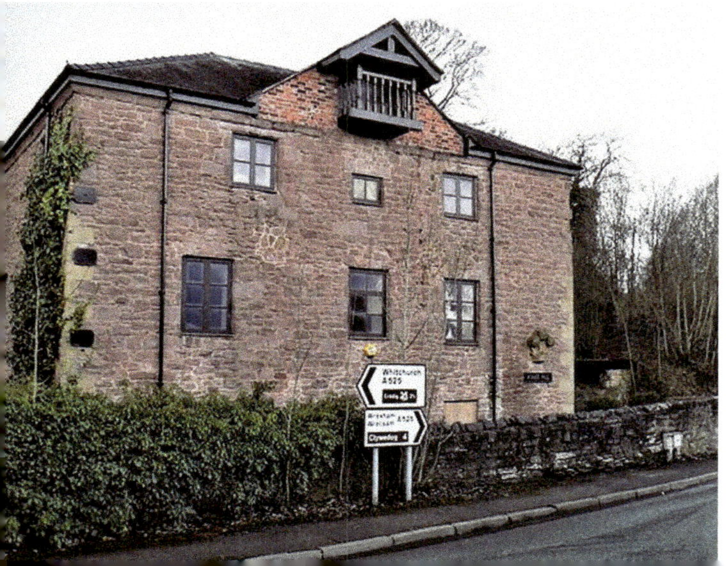

Kings Mills. There had been a mill on this site since at least the fifteen century. The present building is eighteenth century and remained as a mill until 1940.

King Charles

King Charles I twice visited Wrexham in the early days of the Civil War. On the first occasion in September 1642, he addressed the townspeople from the Shire Hall. On the second occasion in October, he visited Richard Lloyd at Bryn-y-Ffynnon Hall. That the King was in Wrexham at all indicates the significance of North Wales to the Royalist cause. Parliamentary sentiment was not unknown in the Wrexham area; however, it was generally regarded as Royalist territory. Sir Thomas Myddelton of Chirk was one of the few local landowners who used his wealth and influence on behalf of Parliament. Interestingly, after the death of Cromwell in 1658, Sir Thomas was part of a plot to restore the monarchy.

Wrexham was not destined to play a particularly significant part in the Civil War as it had no castle, and was open and exposed. In 1642 it was, however, regarded as a convenient place for assemblies and Wrexham was selected as the meeting place for the gentry of Denbighshire and Flintshire. They resolved to raise a regiment of volunteers for the king and subscribed £1,500 for the purpose. Sir Thomas Salisbury was appointed to command the troops. According to Bulstrode Whitelock, Roger Mostyn raised 1,500 men for the king in twelve hours. If this applies to a separate regiment, it implies that Flintshire and Denbigshire alone contributed over 2,000 of the Welshmen who fought at the Battle of Edgehill.

Although Wrexham played no significant part in the Civil War, it did, at various times, become the headquarters of either the Parliamentarians or the Royalists. Following the short-lived battle at Holt Bridge, Parliamentary troops were quartered in the town, some of whom took up residence in the parish church. Here they are said to have broken up an extremely fine organ to use the lead to make ammunition.

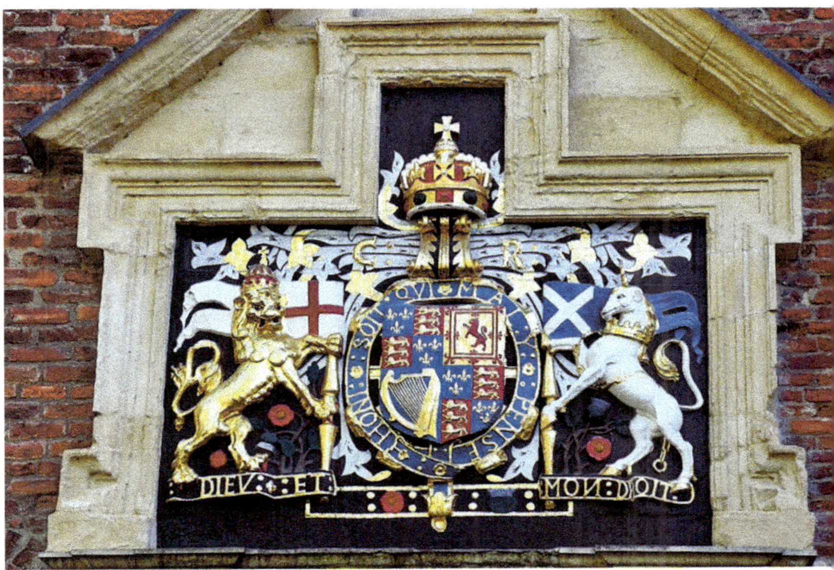

The coat of arms of Charles I.

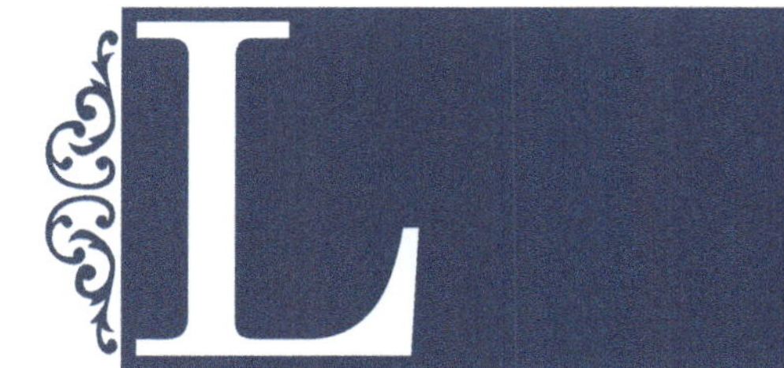

Llangollen Canal

The canal that we know today as the Llangollen Canal was originally known as the Ellesmere Canal, taking its name from Ellesmere in Shropshire, where the plans for the canal were approved. As originally envisaged, the idea was to create a canal from Ellesmere Port to Chester and from Chester, via Wrexham, to Shrewsbury, thus providing a means of easier transshipment of goods, particularly coal, iron ore and clay, between the industries of North Wales and the Midlands. The first stage, from Ellesmere Port to Chester, was completed in 1796. Three more sections were begun in 1794 around Welsh Frankton to serve the coal mines near Chirk and the limestone quarries at Llanymynech. However, in 1800, William Jessop advised that

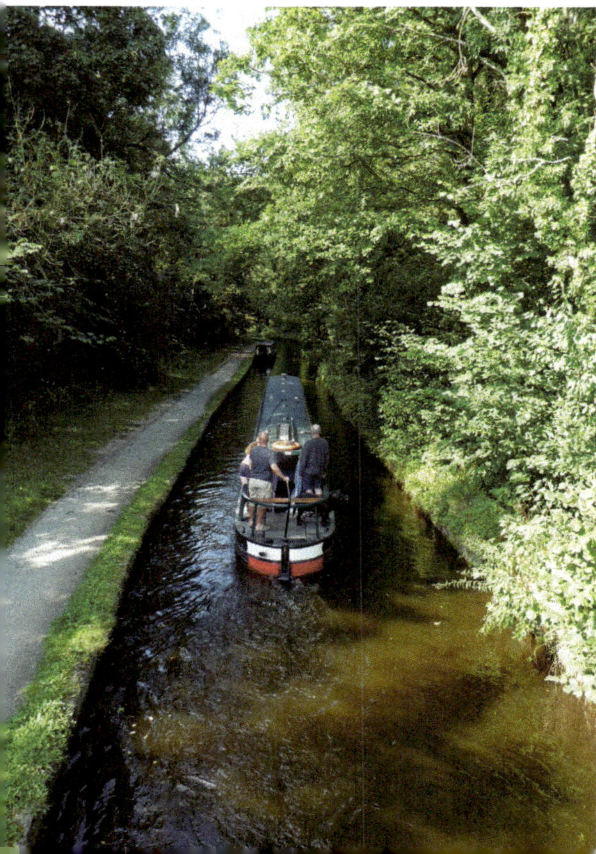

The Llangollen Canal. The relative narrowness of the canal indicates its purpose as a feeder for the Ellesmere Canal.

it was inadvisable to construct a canal between Pontcysyllte and Chester due to the topography of the land. In view of this, it was decided to take the canal through Shropshire to join the Chester & Ellesmere Canal at Hurlstone. The main line of the canal from Hurleston to Trevor was completed in 1805. The decision not to continue the canal to Chester raised problems of water supply, as it had originally been intended to take water from the River Clywedog west of Wrexham. In 1804, work had begun on a narrower, feeder branch, between Trevor and Llantysillio, where could be drawn from the River Dee.

Traffic on the canal peaked in the mid-nineteenth century, carrying coal, iron, limestone, lime, timber, grain and bricks. However, traffic had virtually ceased by the 1930s. The canal survived closure in 1944 mainly because it fed water to the reservoir at Hurleston. Today, the Llangollen Canal is a favourite with boaters, particularly as it has no locks.

Libraries

Libraries in Wrexham can be traced back to 1879, when the first Reading Room and Library was opened in the upper room of the old Town Hall in December of that year. Just over four years later, the library was transferred to the Guildhall in Chester Street. By 1894, the library had outgrown its space at the Guildhall and an appeal was made to the Scottish-American philanthropist Andrew Carnegie. This resulted in a grant of £4,000 for a new building and a further £300 with which to furnish it. The design of the building was put out to tender, and the chosen architect was Vernon Hodge of London. The foundation stone was laid on 1 January 1906 and the building

The Carnegie Library. Built with a grant from Andrew Carnegie, the library was opened in 1907. The library closed in 1973, when the new library and art gallery was opened in Llwyn Isaf.

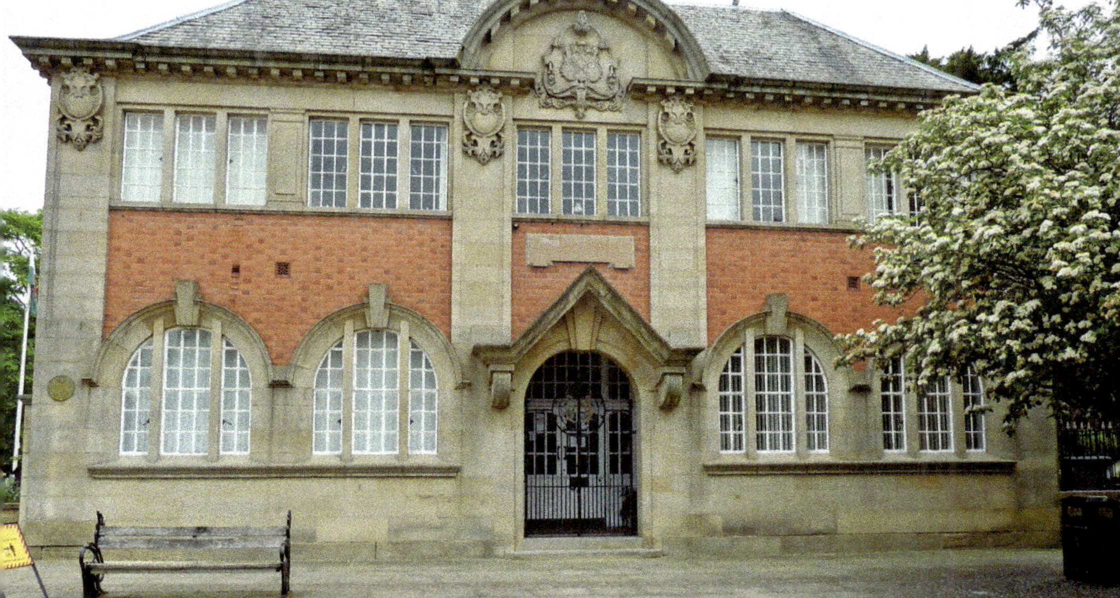

opened just twelve months later in February 1907. Built in Cefn stone, the building is faced with Ruabon terracotta facing brick. Interestingly, the Wrexham library bears a strong resemblance to the Carnegie Library in Pontypool.

The Carnegie Library, as it came to be known, was twice extended, once in 1933 and again in 1951. In 1973, the library and art gallery moved to Llwyn Isaf and was formally opened in 1974. The town police station now occupies what was the art gallery.

Low, William

William Low was a Scottish born surveyor and civil engineer who, at one time, worked with Isambard Kingdom Brunel. He came to Wrexham to work on the Chester–Shrewsbury Railway and he almost certainly knew Henry Robertson, the Chief Engineer for the Chester–Shrewsbury Railway. He became a joint owner of the Vron Colliery in 1850. In 1864, he designed and built a house on Rhosddu Road, in Wrexham, and it was here that he formed the Channel Tunnel Company and drew up the first realistic plans for a tunnel under the channel. Low's design was for a twin bore tunnel with occasional connecting passages to aid airflow. Interestingly, Low's design was not dissimilar to the Channel Tunnel that was actually built. There is a ceramic memorial to William Low's work in Argyle Street, Wrexham. This was erected by the Wrexham Area Civic Society and unveiled by the Duke of Westminster in April 1994, the same year that the Channel Tunnel was opened.

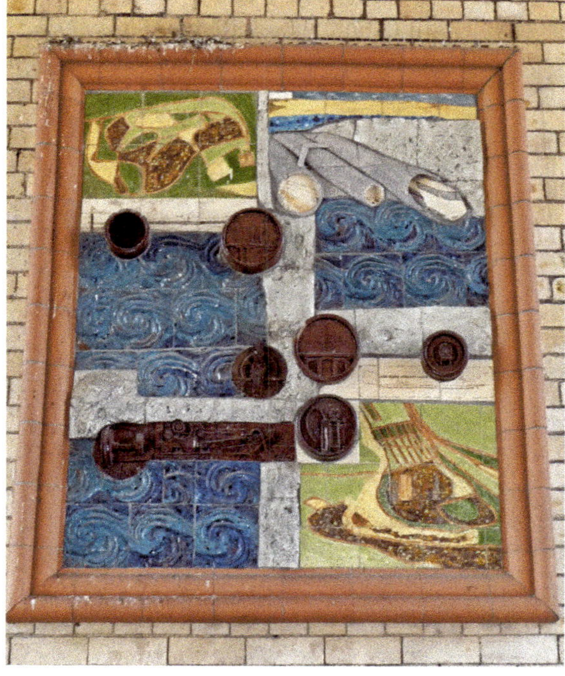

This small memorial to William Low, the Scottish-born surveyor and civil engineer, was erected by the Wrexham Area Civic Society. Low formed the Channel Tunnel Company and drew up the first realistic plans for a tunnel under the English Channel.

Markets

Until the concentration of population into towns and the advent of good transport services, markets and fairs were the most important means of trading. Records show that Wrexham has been a marketplace for its rural hinterland since at least 1331. In the seventeenth century, markets were held on Mondays and Thursdays with stalls in the High Street, Hope Street and Church Street. In 1858, Wrexham Corporation went some way to regularising the markets and designated Thursdays and Saturdays as market days.

Today there are three indoor markets plus the outdoor Monday market in Queens Square. The Butchers' Market, in High Street, in addition to meat offers a wide range of other goods. The General Market is in Henblas Street, and, as the name suggests,

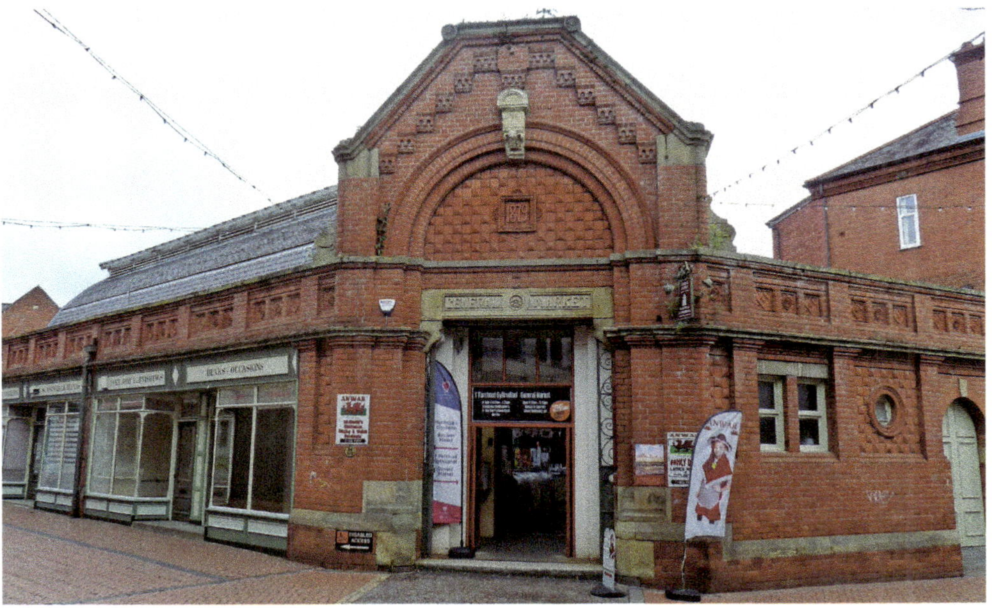

Wrexham General Market, Henblas Street. Opened in 1879, the main entrance (seen here) is of red Ruabon brick with freestone dressings and terracotta enrichments.

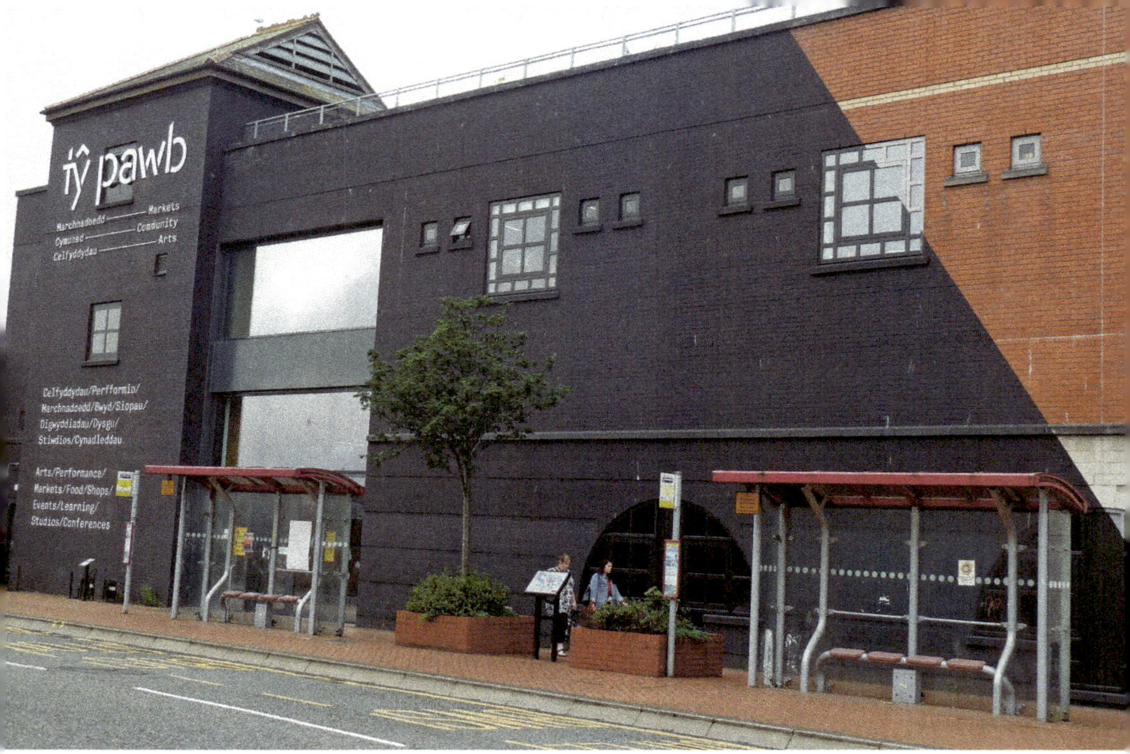

Above: Ty Pawb, Market Street, is Wrexham's latest regeneration project. The former Peoples' Market has now been turned into an art gallery, performing space, market and food hall.

Below: Wrexham Monday market. For a great many years, Wrexham was the market centre for the surrounding area. The small Monday market is the last vestige of a long tradition that reflects the ways in which shopping habits have changed.

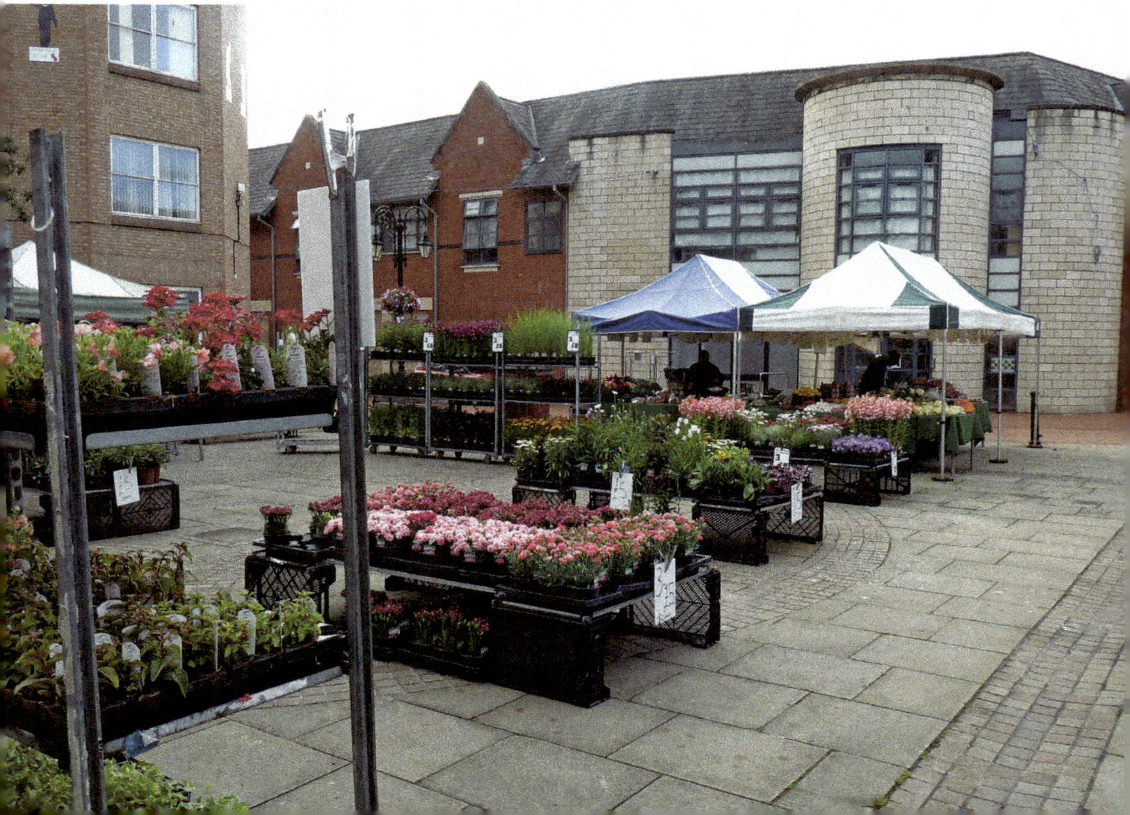

offers a wide range of goods. The People's Market (Ty Pawb) is in Chester Street and combines an indoor market, food hall and art gallery. More recently, in April 2022, a street market was organised for the first Saturday each month.

Museum

Wrexham Museum and Archives are housed in what was once known as County Buildings, in Regent Street. The building was a militia barracks until 1879, when it became the town's magistrates' court and police headquarters. The police moved out to their new headquarters at Bodhyfryd in 1976 and two years later, in 1978, the magistrates' court also moved to a new building in Bodhyfryd. The building then became part of the Wrexham College of Art and Design until 1995, when it was taken over by Wrexham Council as the town's museum. The building was extensively redeveloped in 1996–97. Today, the museum houses an excellent collection of artefacts relating to both Wrexham and the surrounding area.

Wrexham Museum is housed in the former County Buildings in Regents Street. The building was originally a militia barracks before becoming the town magistrates' court and police station.

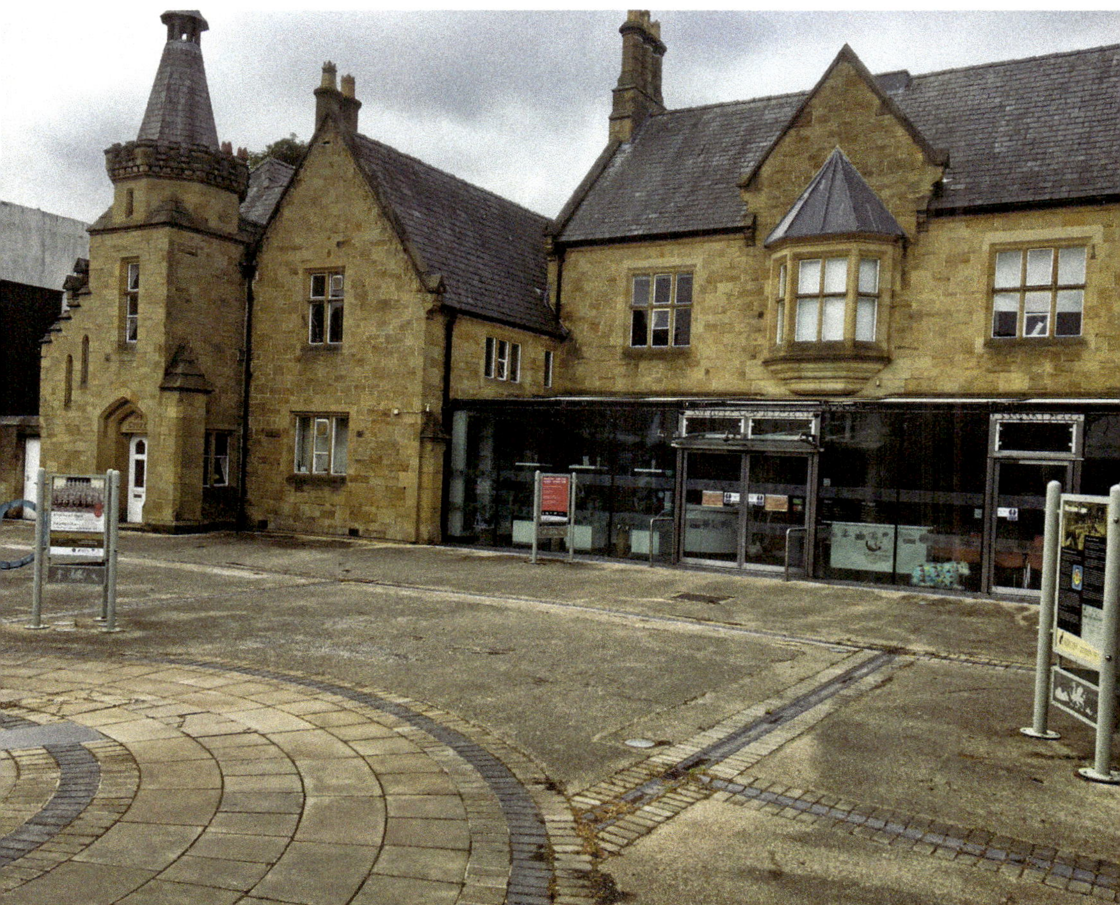

Millenium Mural

The Wrexham Millennium Mural is on the south wall of the library. This is a ceramic mural based on Wrexham past and present. Designed by the artist Penny Hampson, the mural measures some 900 cm x 500 cm. The scenes on the mural have been made using terracotta tiles produced at the Dennis of Ruabon Tile and Brick Factory. The mural is the result of work by children aged three to eleven from eight different schools in Wrexham.

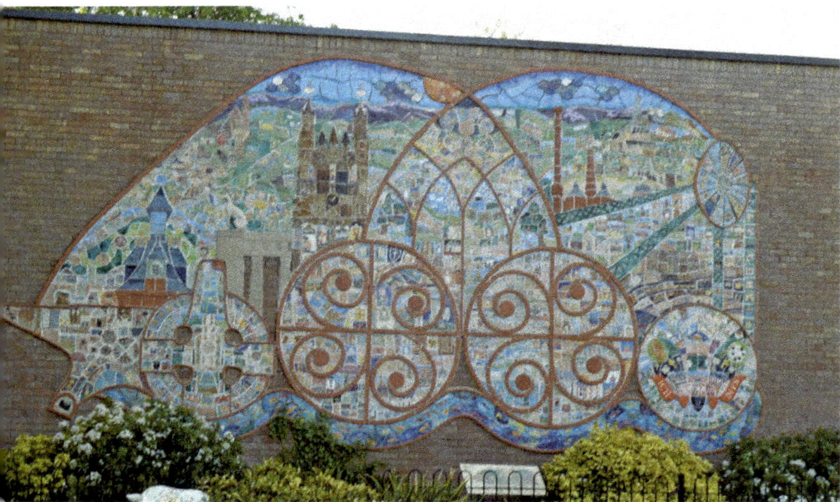

The Millennium Mural. This ceramic mural is on the wall of the town library in Llwyn Isaf. Designed by Penny Hampson, the various parts of the mural were completed by children from Wrexham schools.

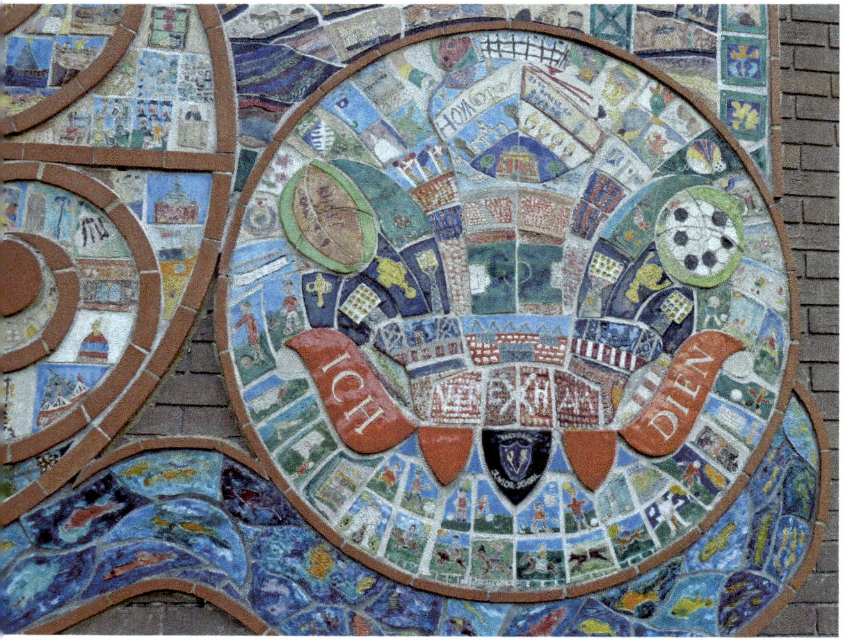

Millenium Mural detail.

Miners' Institute, Rhosllannerchrugog

The Rhos Miners' Institute was opened in 1926, the same year as the General Strike. It was built at a cost of £18,000 by the Miners' Welfare Organisation who levied 1*d* a ton on extracted coal between 1924 and 1926. The institute was supported and run on a daily basis by a subscription of 2*d* a week from the wages of the miners, who managed to raise another £20,000. For fifty years, the institute was the social and cultural centre of Rhos and the surrounding villages. The institute closed in 1977 and was purchased by the council, who, in 1985, decided to demolish the building due to its poor condition. However, a local campaign saved the building and, at a cost of £4.3 million, it was reopened in 1999 as the Stiwt Theatre. Today, the Stiwt is a successful theatre and meeting place and, during the course of the year, offers a wide programme of both professional and amateur performances.

In 2007, the Stiwt clock, whose chimes had raised the miners for their shifts at the Hafod Colliery, ceased to work. An appeal was launched in 2018 to repair it, and, from a variety of sources, some £1000,00 was raised. This provided sufficient funds to restore the whole front of the building, as well as the clock ,which was working again by May 2019.

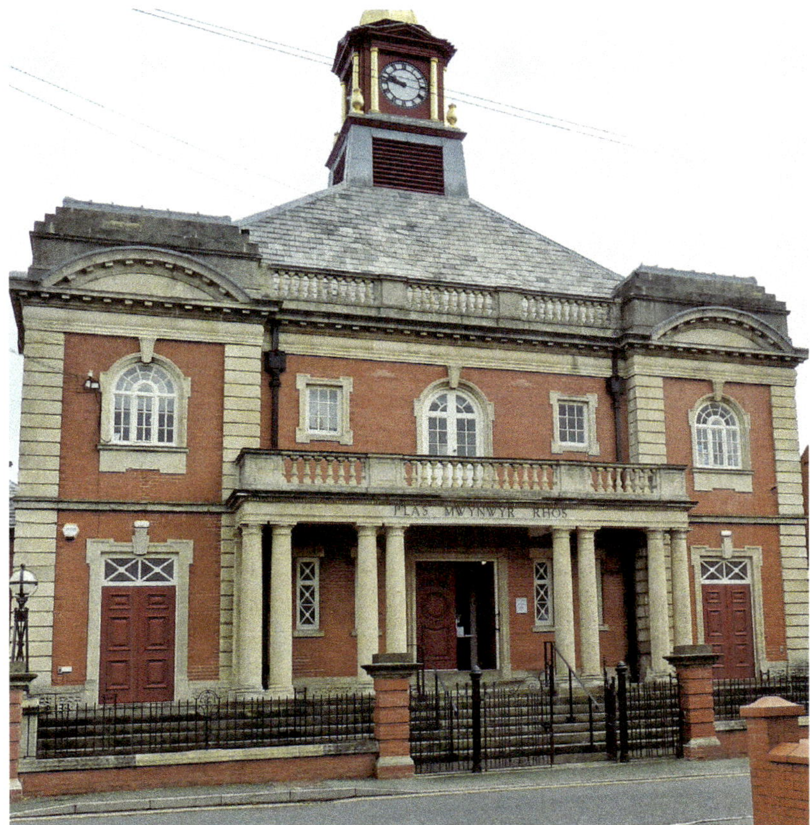

The Former Miners' Institute, Rhos. Built in 1926, it is now the Stiwt Theatre.

National Eisteddfod

The National Eisteddfod of Wales has been held in Wrexham on five occasions. The first of these was in 1876, in a pavilion erected just off Hill Street. The Eisteddfod returned to Wrexham in 1888 and on this occasion the event was attended by Prime Minister W. E. Gladstone. The 1912 Eisteddfod was also held in Wrexham and was visited by David Lloyd George, the then Chancellor of the Exchequer, who was heckled

The Gorsedd Stones, Acton Park. The last occasion that the National Eisteddfod was held in Wrexham was in 1977, when it was held on Borras Airfield. The proclamation ceremony for the eisteddfod was held in Acton Park, where the stones can still be seen.

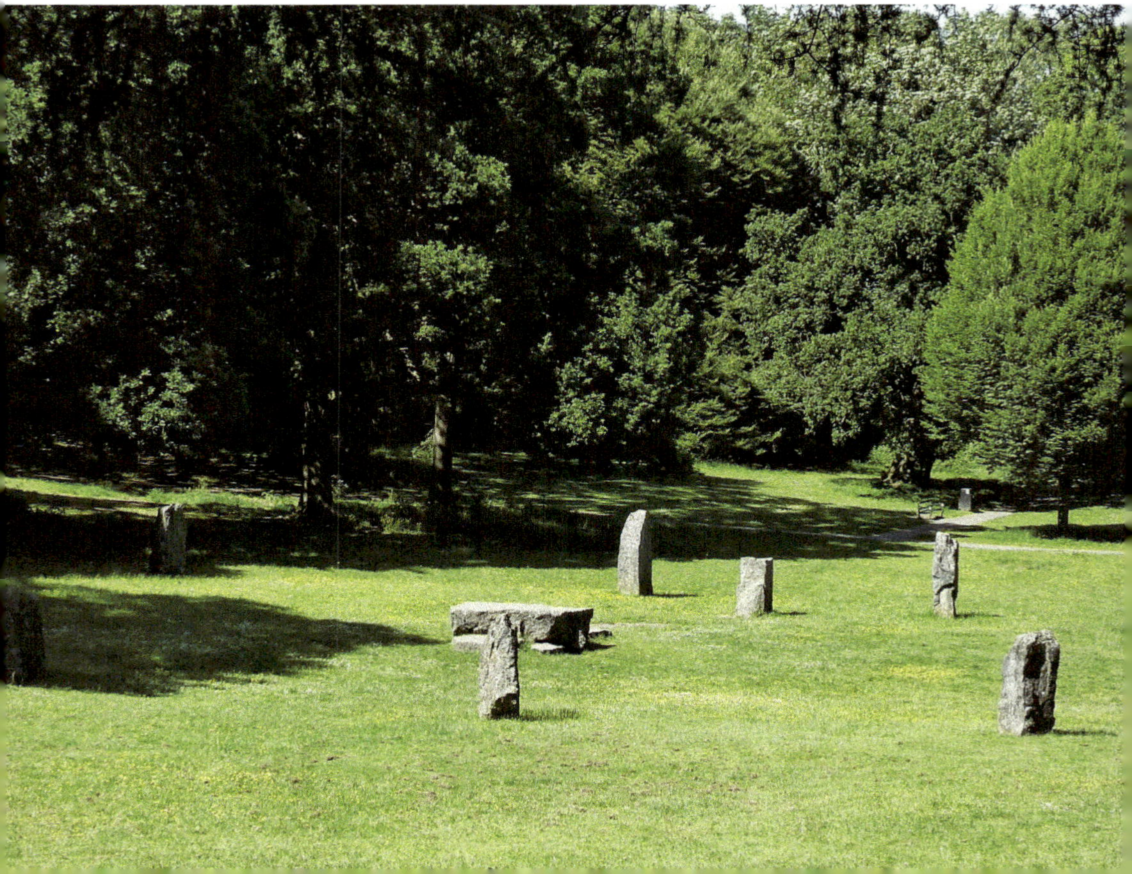

and stoned by a group of suffragettes. 1933 saw the Eisteddfod back in Wrexham, and on this occasion it was held in the Parciau. The last occasion on which the Eisteddfod came to Wrexham was in 1977, when it was held on Borras Airfield. The proclamation ceremony for the Eisteddfod, which was held in July 1976, took place in Acton Park, where the Gorsedd Stones can still be seen.

Nonconformist Chapels

Nonconformity grew in Wales during the eighteenth and nineteenth centuries and, by the middle of the nineteenth century, Wales was predominantly a Nonconformist country, particularly in industrial areas where Nonconformist religion was popular, with many chapels being built by the different denominations. The Welsh Methodist revival of the eighteenth century was a significant factor in the history of the country. The revival began in the Church of England in Wales, partly as a reaction to the neglect generally felt in Wales at the hands of absentee bishops and clergy. Although the revival of the eighteenth century was centred on the Methodist church, it also influenced the older Nonconformist churches such as the Baptists and the Congregationalists.

In Wrexham, the English Congregationalists originally met in a house in Chapel Street (Pen-y-Bryn). In 1789, they built a chapel in the same street, in what the National Monuments Record calls the 'Sub Classical style'. The building was modified between 1816 and 1818 and extensively remodelled in 1881. The Congregationalists were a Puritan denomination that grew out of the Reformation of the sixteenth century. In the seventeenth century, Congregationalists dominated the membership of Cromwell's New Model Army. In 1898, the Congregationalists moved out of their chapel to a new building in Salisbury Road, which is now known as the United Reformed Church. The Welsh Baptists now moved into the vacated building in Chapel Street. The Welsh Baptists were an offshoot of the wider Baptist movement. In 1904 there started what was to become the last Revival in Wales; this was essentially a Nonconformist and Welsh language phenomenon. In January 1905, the *Seven Cymru* newspaper reported that, in Wrexham, 'The spirit of Revival is not as strong as in Glamorgan as most of the town are not Welsh speaking.' This was not the case in nearby, Welsh speaking Rhos, where the revival was particularly strong.

While there are numerous Nonconformist chapels in Wrexham, one that tends to draw the attention of the visitor is Trinity Presbyterian Church in King Street. This church community was originally established in 1845 in a building in Abbot Street before building a church in Hill Street in 1857. Some fifty years later, the church community secured land at the corner of King Street and Rhosddu Road on which to build a new church. This imposing new church was designed by W. Beddoe Rees of Cardiff and built by local builder T. L. Davies of Rhos, and was officially opened in October 1908. Not unusually for a Presbyterian church, a school room capable of holding 250 was included in the design. Interestingly, during the Second World War, the school room was pressed into service as a reception centre for evacuees from Liverpool, an extra classroom for Grove Park Girls School and a hospital for elderly ladies from the east end of London.

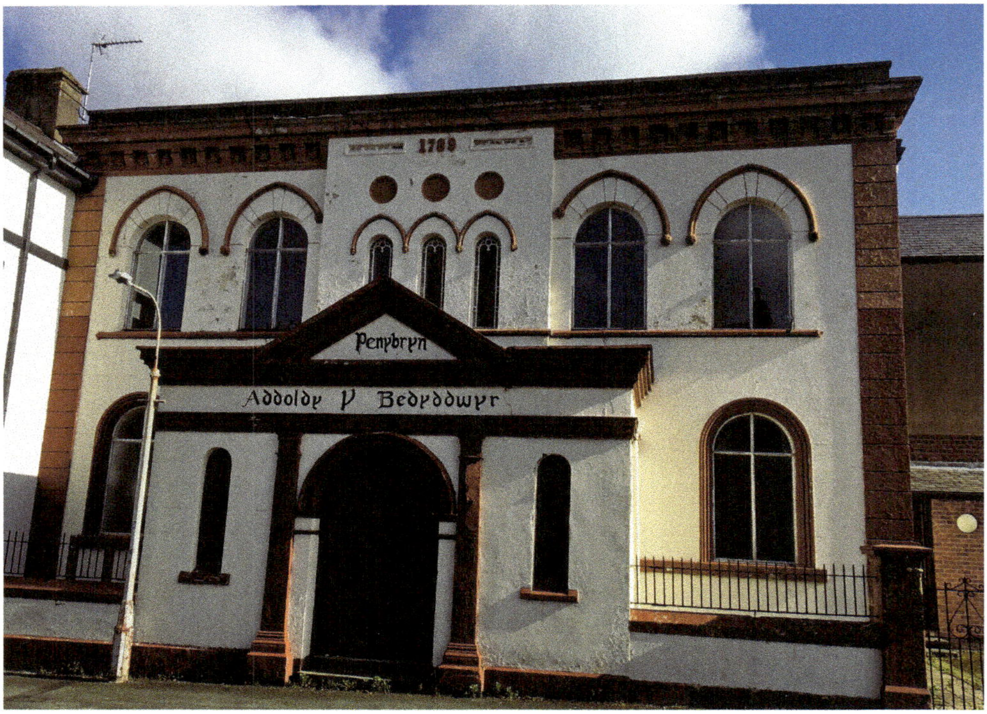

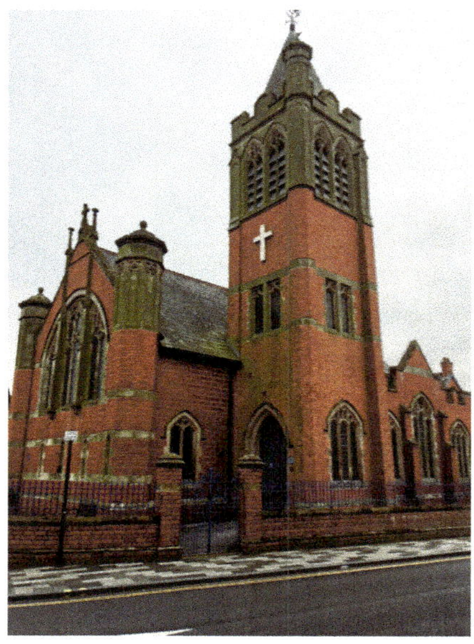

Above: The Welsh Baptist chapel, Pen-y-Bryn. Dating from 1789, the chapel was modified between 1816 and 1818 and extensively remodelled in 1881.

Left: Trinity Presbyterian church, King Street. Opened in 1908, the church was designed by W. Beddoe Rees.

Offa's Dyke

Offa's Dyke was probably built in the late eight century on the orders of Offa, King of Mercia. The Offa's Dyke Path is a long-distance walking route which runs for 177 miles from Chepstow on the Severn Estuary to Prestatyn on the North Wales coast. The path, which was opened in July 1971, crosses the English-Welsh border some twenty times, and celebrates its fiftieth birthday in 2021. For a number of reasons the path does not always directly follow the dyke. North of Llangollen, for example, the path goes westward into the Clwydian Hills, rather than eastwards to follow the

One of the many way markers on the Offa's Dyke Path. This 177-mile, long-distance walking route celebrated its fiftieth birthday in 2021.

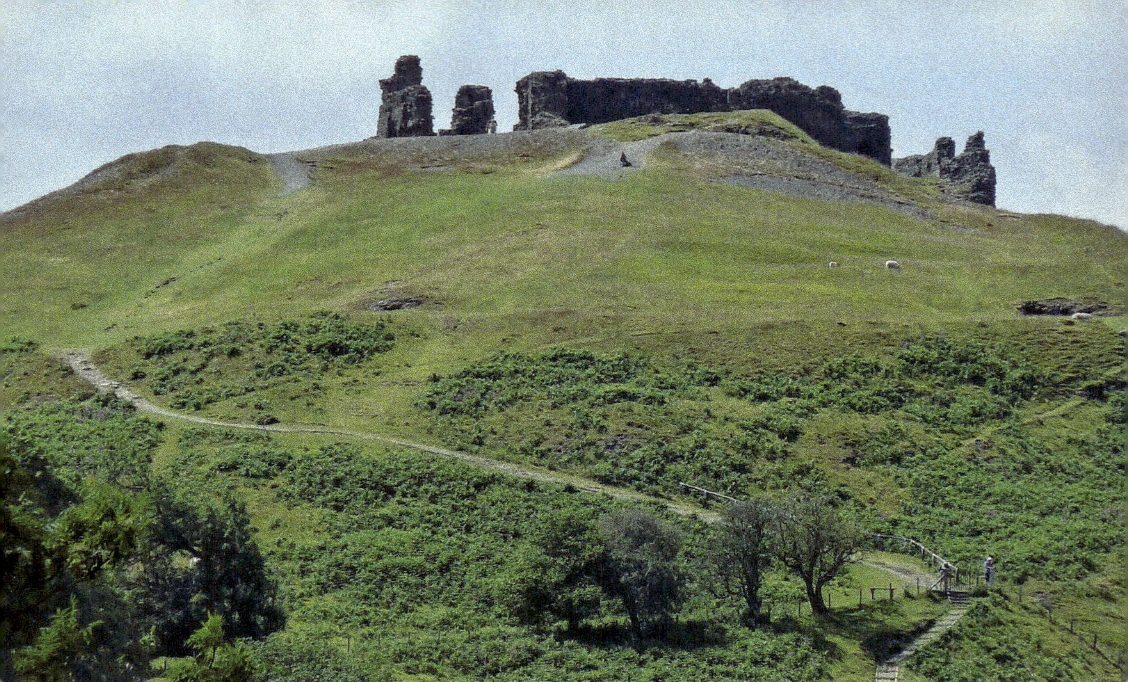

Castell Dinas Bran from the Offa's Dyke Path. Castell Dinas Bran was possibly built by Gruffydd Maelor II around 1260, although there were certainly earlier structures on this hilltop site.

dyke through the suburbs of Wrexham. Interestingly, the village of Johnstown is built on Offa's Dyke. In the Wrexham area, the official route of the Offa's Dyke Path skirts around the Chirk Castle estate. However, when the castle is open to the public, walkers are allowed to follow the dyke to Home Farm. The dyke is actually under the lake at Chirk. The two routes meet again at Tyn-y-Groes and follow downhill paths to the A5. In the Dee Valley the path divides again; the lower route takes walkers along the B5434 and over the Dee via the stone bridge. The higher route takes walkers over Pontcysyllte Aqueduct. Having reached Trevor, the path then takes walkers through Trevor Hall woods to the Panorama Walk and Castell Dinas Bran. The route then heads towards Llandegla and onwards to the Clwydian Range.

Old Registry

The Grade II listed Old Registry in Chester Store is one of the few recognisably eighteenth-century buildings in the town. According to A. N. Palmer, a house existed on this site in 1727 and it appears to have been remodelled in the later eighteenth century. Over the years, it had a number of owners until, in the early twentieth century, it housed the St Giles' Home for Children. During the First World War, the house was used to house Belgian refugees from Antwerp and Malines. After the war, in the 1920s, the office of the Registrar of Births Marriages and Deaths moved into the house, and remained there until 1978. The building is currently given over to commercial use.

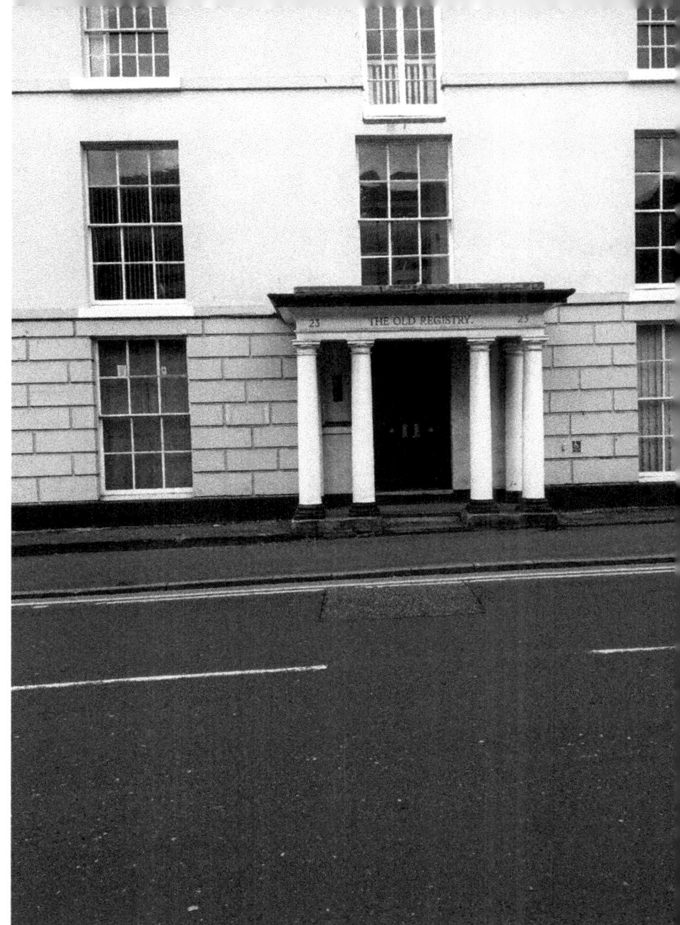

The Old Registry, Chester Street.
An excellent example of an
eighteenth-century town house
now given over to commercial use.

Overton-on-Dee

The town of Overton-on-Dee lies 7 miles from Wrexham and its small size belies its importance in the early history of the area. It was first recorded in 1195 and in the twelfth century Madog ap Maredudd built a castle here. Edward I granted Overton a weekly market and annual fair in 1279 and it became a borough by royal charter in 1292. Two years later, in 1294, the new borough was to become one of the first targets in Madog ap Llywelyn's revolt against English rule.

Overton is now a Conservation Area and has a significant number of interesting eighteenth- and nineteenth-century buildings, many of which are listed. Although there is no market now, its wide main street testifies to its earlier role as a market town. The church of St Mary the Virgin is famed for its twenty-one yew trees, some of which are thought to be between 1,500 and 2,000 years old. Certainly they probably predate the church. There was a church here in the twelfth century but the major part of the present building probably dates from the 1450s.

Although it is now in the County Borough of Wrexham, Overton was, for many years, an enclave of Flintshire known as Maelor Saesneg (English Maelor).

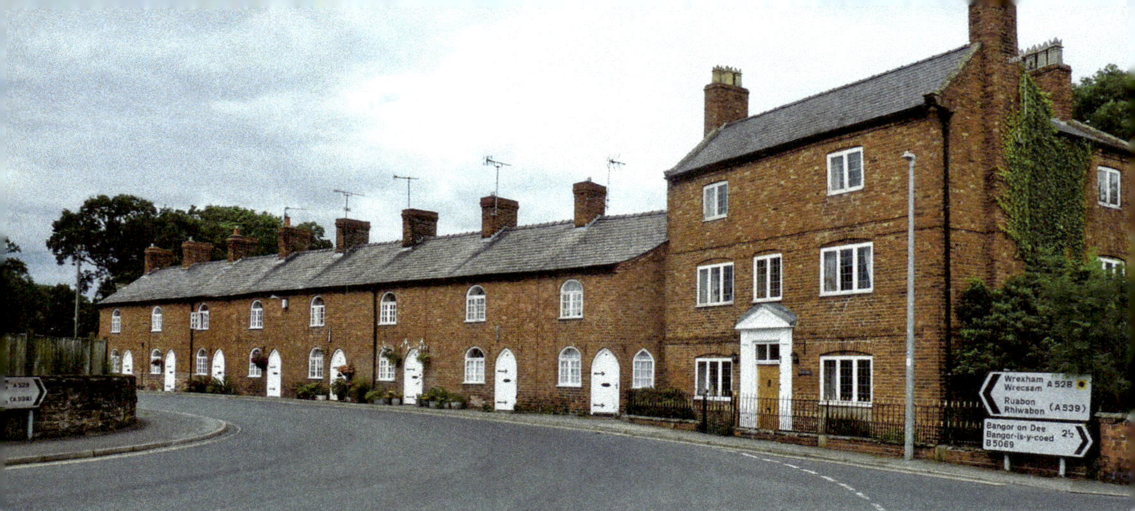

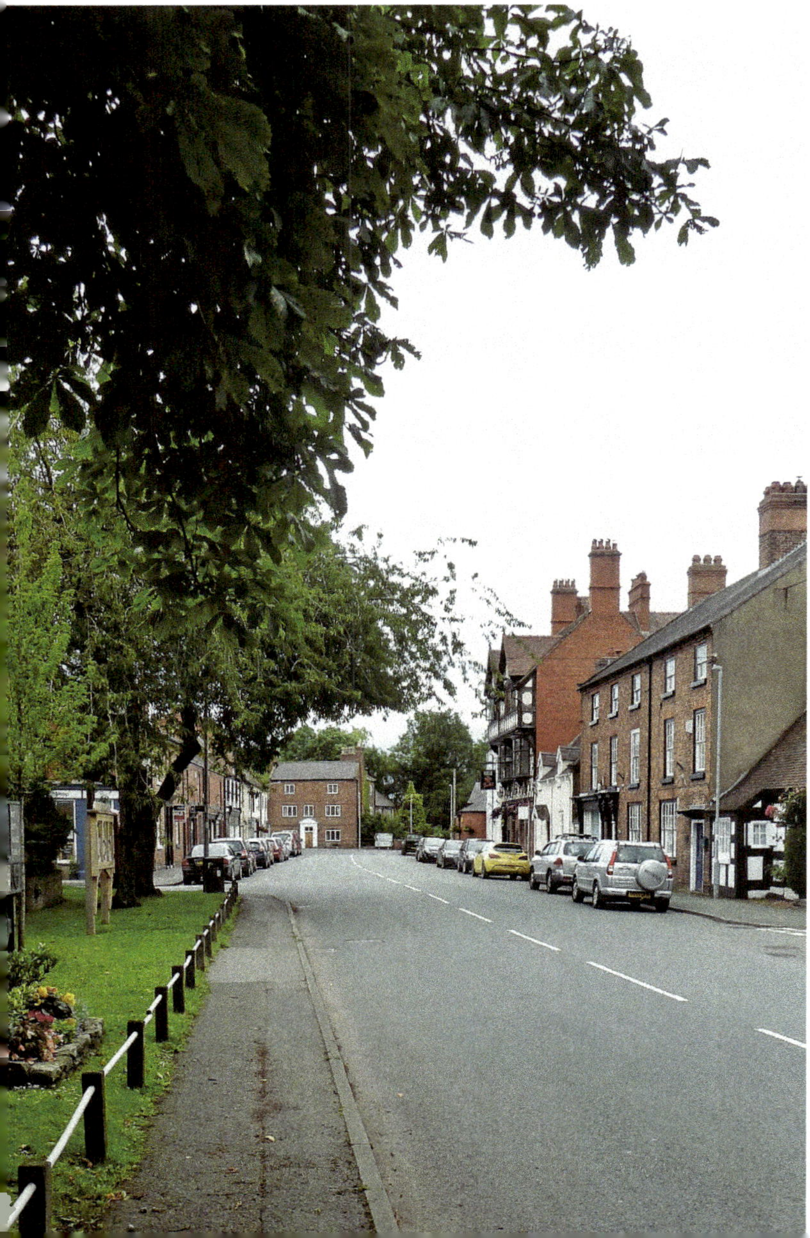

Above: Overton on Dee. Although now part of Wrexham County Borough, Overton was originally in an enclave of the traditional county of Flintshire known as Maelor Saesneg (English Maelor).

Left: Overton on Dee. Overton is a medieval settlement that became a borough by royal charter in 1292.

Overton Arcade

Overton Arcade is a short glass-covered thoroughfare leading from High Street to Temple Row. It was built in 1868 by William Overton from whom it takes its name.

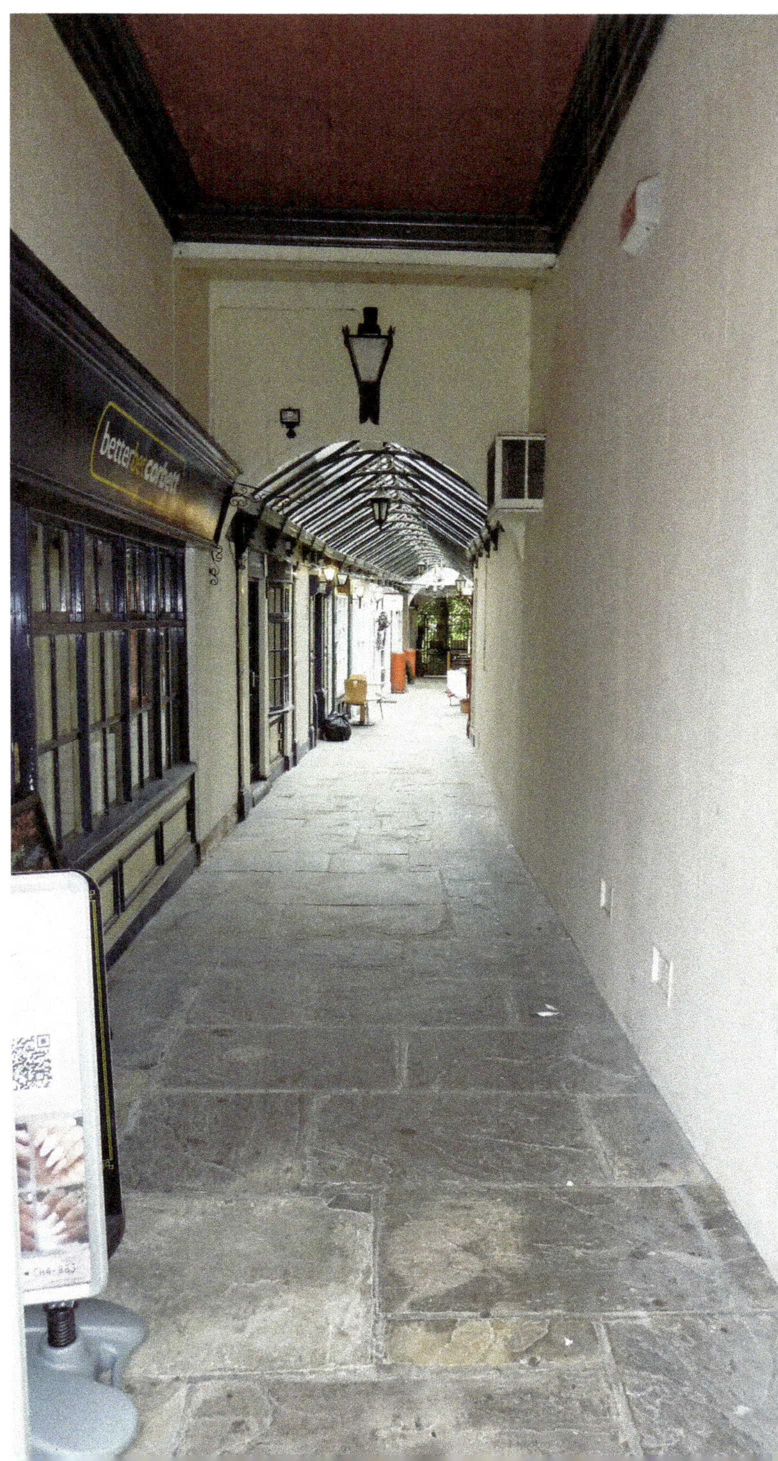

Overton Arcade, High Street, Wrexham. This small arcade was built in 1868 by William Overton.

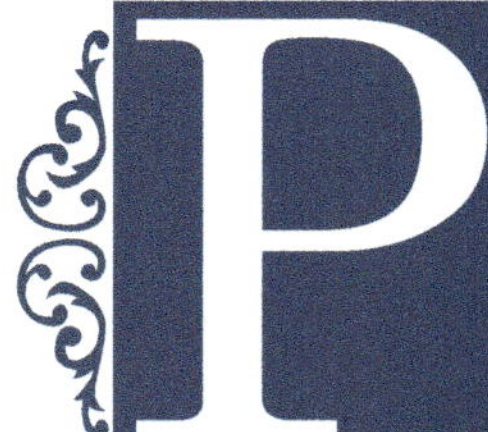# Pubs

As with most market towns, Wrexham could boast a good number of pubs. In the 1830s there were some forty-nine pubs in the town serving a population of just 6,000. From the nineteenth-century Trade Directories, it is possible to trace over 150 pub names in Wrexham. This does not, of course, mean that there were 150 pubs at any one time,

The Horse & Jockey pub, Hope Street, a rare thatched building in an urban setting. Possibly a sixteenth-century open hall house, it was later subdivided into three cottages. It became a single building again in 1860, when it was converted into a pub.

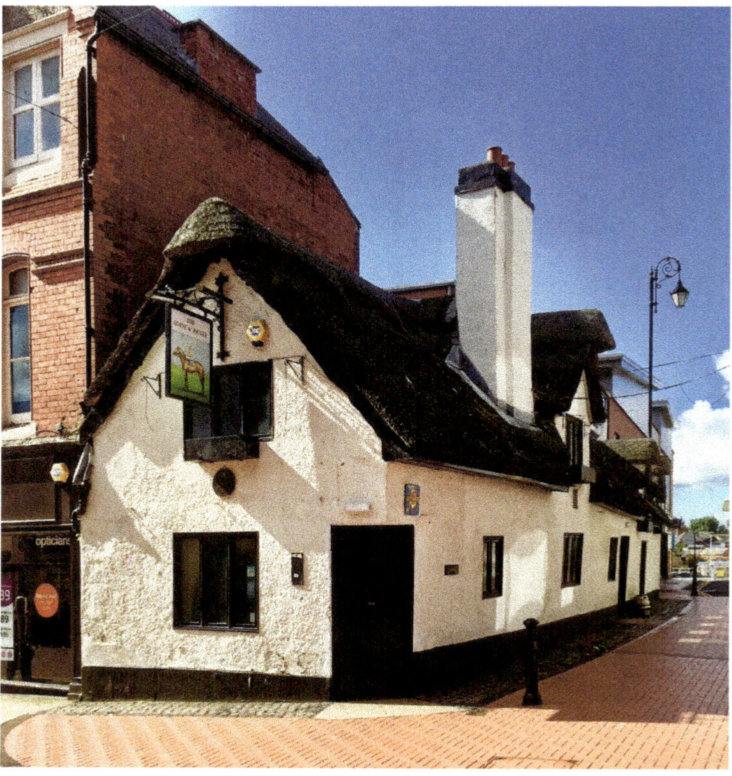

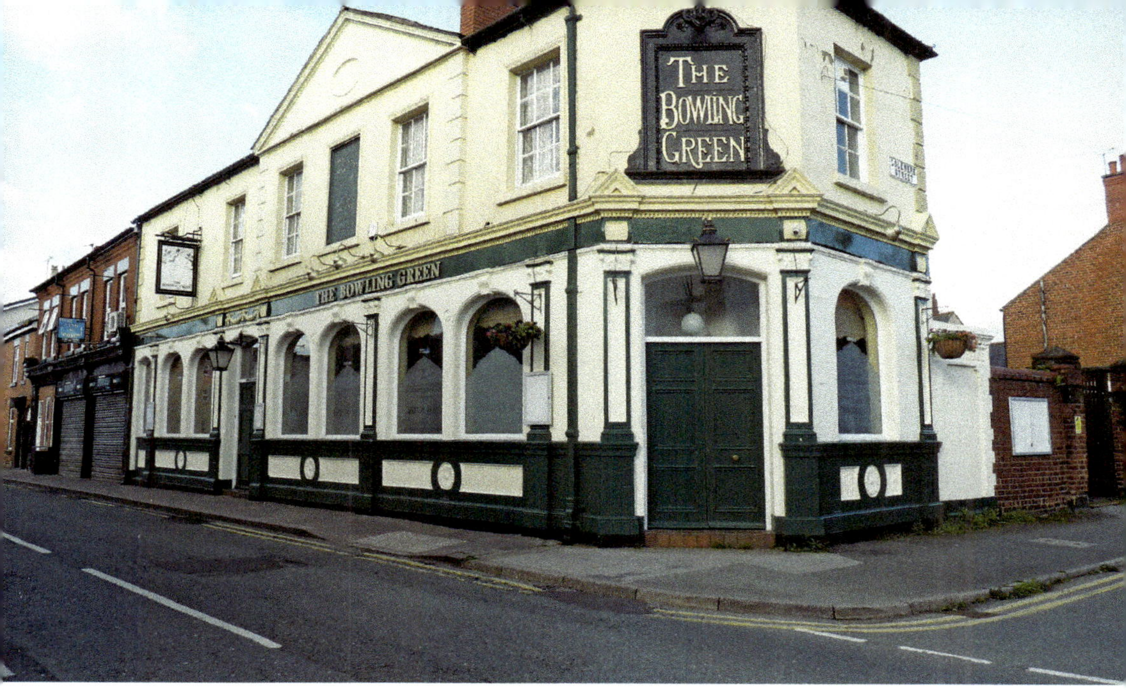

The Bowling Green pub, Pen-y-Bryn, a good example of Victorian pub architecture.

but reflects changes in pub names and some pubs closing and others opening. The Feathers, for example, in Chester Street was, at various times, The Plume of Feathers and the Prince of Wales. The Wynnstay Arms was also known as The George, Spread Eagles, Eagles and Three Spread Eagles. A great number of these pubs have now been lost to redevelopment. One of the older pub buildings in the town was the Horse and Jockey in Hope Street. The configuration of this thatched building suggests that it started life as a sixteenth-century open hall house. Certainly, it was later divided into three cottages before being combined into a single building in 1860 and becoming a pub. It was named after Fred Archer, the jockey, who rode at Bangor-on-Dee. The Horse and Jockey is often referred to as the oldest pub in Wrexham. Unfortunately, this is not the case, as there is no reference to the building as a pub before 1860.

Police

Policing in Wrexham can be traced back to the County Police Act of 1839, which allowed for the establishment of a police force in Denbighshire. Prior to this, any policing would have been carried out by the parish constables, who were appointed by the annual parish vestry meeting. A Superintendent and four constables were based in Wrexham. Following the militia move to Hightown Barracks in 1877, the police moved into County Buildings.

In 1975, the police moved from their old station at County Buildings in Regent Street into a new purpose built HQ at Bodhyfryd. The new building was designed by the Denbighshire County Architect Eric Langford Lewis in what CADW would later describe as 'a rare and unusual slab and podium design'. The fourteen storey,

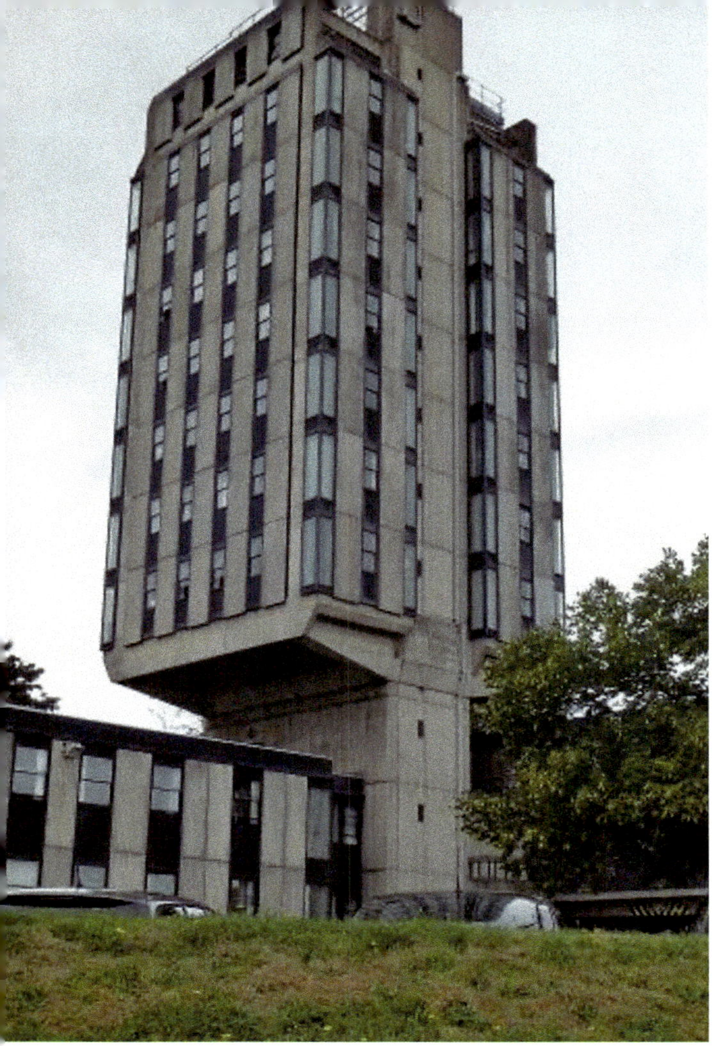

Left: The former police HQ at Bodhyfryd. The 140-foot-tall slab and podium building was demolished in 2020.

Below: Wrexham's new police station is housed in the former art gallery.

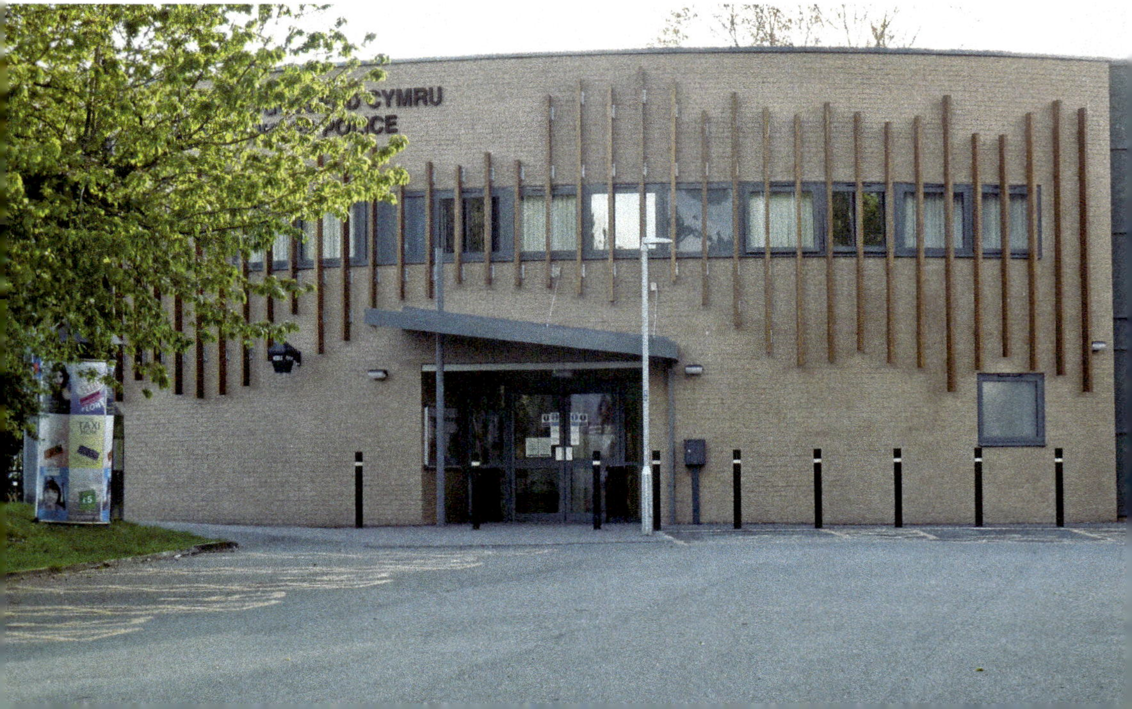

140-foot building was the tallest building in Wrexham since the building of St Giles' Tower in the fifteenth century. The building dominated the Wrexham skyline for some forty years but, eventually, outlived its usefulness. A new Eastern Command HQ and custody facility was built at Llay and the police moved out of the Bodhyfrd building in 2019. In order to maintain a police presence in Wrexham, a new town station was established in the old art gallery of the library. Despite being built in a Brutalist style, many local people retained an affection for the 1970s building, and attempts were made to have it listed. The architectural writer and architectural critic Jonathan Glancey described the building as 'Distinctive and Assertive'. However, CADW considered that the building did not meet the criteria for listing, and it was demolished in November 2020.

Parry-Thomas

John Godfrey Parry-Thomas was born in Wrexham in April 1884 and has the singular distinction of being the first driver to be killed in pursuit of the land speed record. His father was curate of Rhosddu church and the family moved to Oswestry in 1889, where Parry-Thomas went to Oswestry School. He then studied engineering at the City & Guilds College in London. He became chief engineer of Leyland Motors but resigned his post to become a full-time racing driver and engineer in 1920. He was quite successful on the racing circuit, winning thirty-eight races in five seasons. In 1925, he switched his attention to the land speed record and acquired the Higham Special. He rebuilt the car with a new body and improved aerodynamics. In 1926, he took his car, which he now called *Babs*, to Pendine Sands where Malcolm Campbell had made his runs in 1924 and 1925. Parry-Thomas recorded a speed of 170 mph, which stood for a year. In March 1927, he was back at Pendine in an attempt to regain his record, which had been beaten by Campbell just weeks earlier. On this occasion, the car rolled and Parry-Thomas was killed. The car was buried in the sand where it remained until it was recovered in 1969 and underwent a fifteen-year restoration programme.

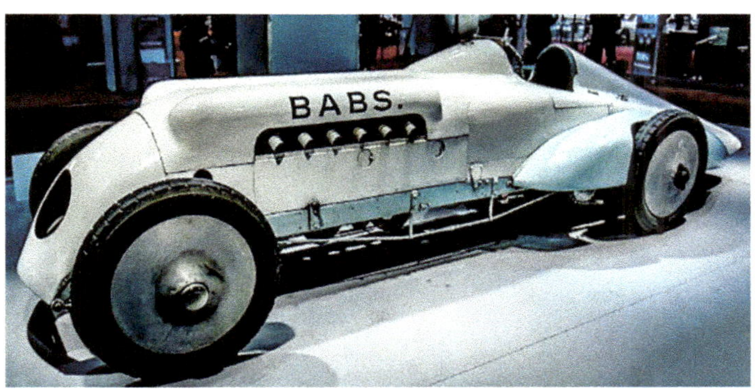

Parry-Thomas was born in Wrexham in April 1884. He was killed when his car overturned during another attempt on the land speed record in 1927.

Queen Victoria

In August 1889, Queen Victoria visited a number of places in North Wales, including Wrexham. This was not her first visit to the area as she had stayed at Wynnstay Park as Princess Victoria. On 24 August the Queen, accompanied by Prince and Princess Henry of Battenberg, travelled from Bala to Ruabon by train, and from there to Wrexham by coach. The Queen received an enthusiastic welcome in Wrexham and, following lunch, proceeded to Acton Park, escorted by the Denbighshire Hussars. In front of a large crowd, numerous speeches were made by Wrexham and Denbighshire dignitaries, choirs sang many patriotic songs and poems were read; during the proceedings the Mayor of Wrexham was knighted. The royal party then returned to Palé, near Bala.

In November 1903, the chairman of the Wrexham Science and Arts Committee announced that Henry Price, a former pupil of the Wrexham College of Art, had been commissioned to produce a bronze statue of Queen Victoria, which was to be placed in front of the RM Academy Woolwich. Price had offered to supply Wrexham with a replica of the statue, if the town could fund the bronze and the casting, which was estimated at £210. It was agreed that this should go ahead, and that the statue would be placed in front of the Carnegie Library. However, it was later decided to place the statue in Guildhall Square, Chester Street.

Despite considerable difficulties in raising the necessary money, the statue was finally in Wrexham by October 1904 and was unveiled by the Mayoress, Mrs Birkett Evans, in May 1905. The statue was moved to its present position in Bellevue Park in the 1960s. It has been said that the statue was erected to mark the coronation of Edward VII. Given that Edward's coronation was in 1902, and the first proposal for the statue was not made until late 1903, this seems an unlikely suggestion.

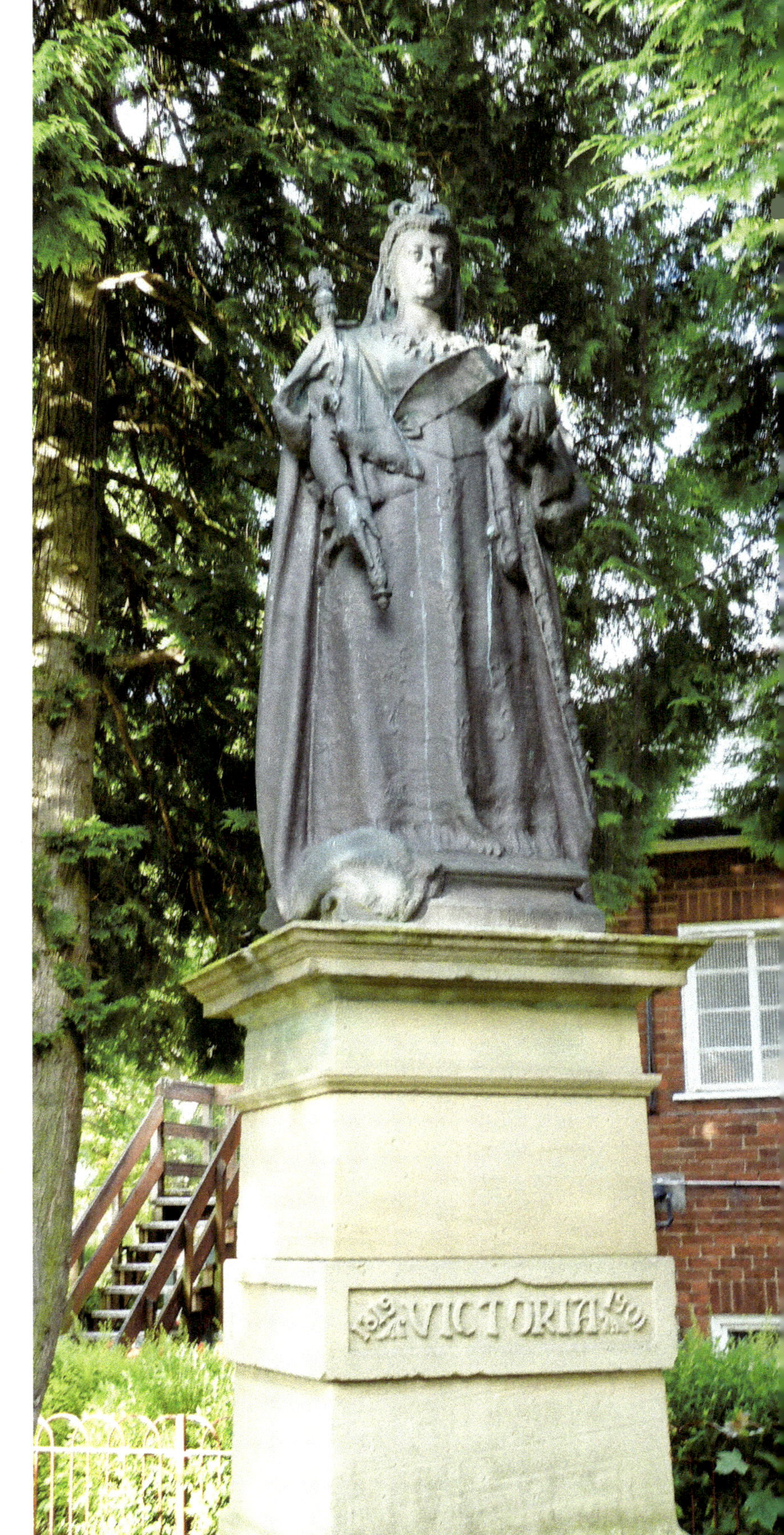

The statue of Queen Victoria in Bellevue Park. Unveiled in 1905, the statue originally stood in front of the old Guildhall in Chester Street before being moved to its present position in the 1960s.

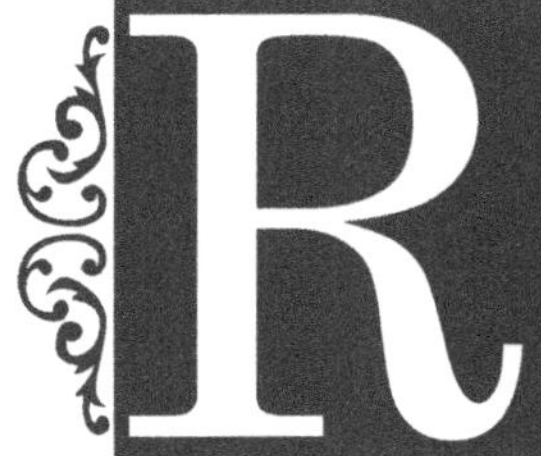

Railways

The Industrial Revolution came to Wrexham long before the railways and it is probable that the decision not to continue the Ellesmere Canal through Wrexham provided impetus for railway development. The failure to carry out the original plan for the Ellesmere Canal meant that coal from the Wrexham area had to make a roundabout journey of 60 miles to Chester, which lay but 14 miles away in the opposite direction. Plans were drawn up as early as 1838 to connect Chester with Ruabon. However, it was not until 1844 that the North Wales Mineral Railway came into existence with the intention of building a railway from Wrexham to Chester, with a branch from Wrexham to Brymbo. A year later, the Shrewsbury, Oswestry & Cheshire Junction Railway was formed. In 1846, these two railways merged to become the Shrewsbury & Chester Railway. From this beginning, an extensive network of freight lines spread out connecting Wrexham to most of the remaining collieries and steelworks in the area. In 1854, the Shrewsbury & Chester Railway became part of the Great Western Railway.

Wrexham General station was opened in 1846 by the Shrewsbury & Chester Railway. Local architect Thomas Penson designed the station in a Jacobean style with Dutch gable pediments. Unusually, in an area known for its red brick, the GWR rebuilt the station in 1912 in the French Pavilion style using stone from the original building.

Until the 1980s, what is now platform 4 of Wrexham General was known as Wrexham Exchange station, which was opened in 1866 for the Wrexham Mold & Connah's Quay Railway. The station was then taken over by the Great Central Railway and, in 1921, changed hands again, becoming part of the London & North Eastern Railway.

The original Wrexham Central station was opened in 1887 by the Wrexham Mould & Connah's Quay Railway, being more convenient for the town centre than Wrexham Exchange station. In 1895, the Wrexham & Ellesmere Railway was formed with financial assistance from the WM&CQR and the Cambrian Railway. This line also ran from Wrexham Central. The Ellesmere line was closed to passenger traffic in 1962. The original Wrexham Central station was much bigger than the single line that exists today. In fact, it covered most of what is now Island Green Shopping Centre. Now an unmanned station, it provides services to Bidston and Liverpool.

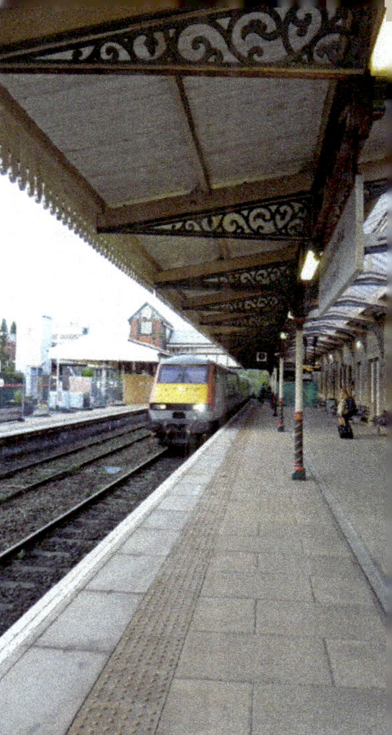

Right: Wrexham General railway station. Opened in 1846 by the Great Western Railway, the station was rebuilt in 1912 in what has been described as the 'French Pavilion' style.

Below: Wrexham Central railway station at Island Green. While still an active station, it is only a fraction of its former size and serves the Wrexham–Bidston line.

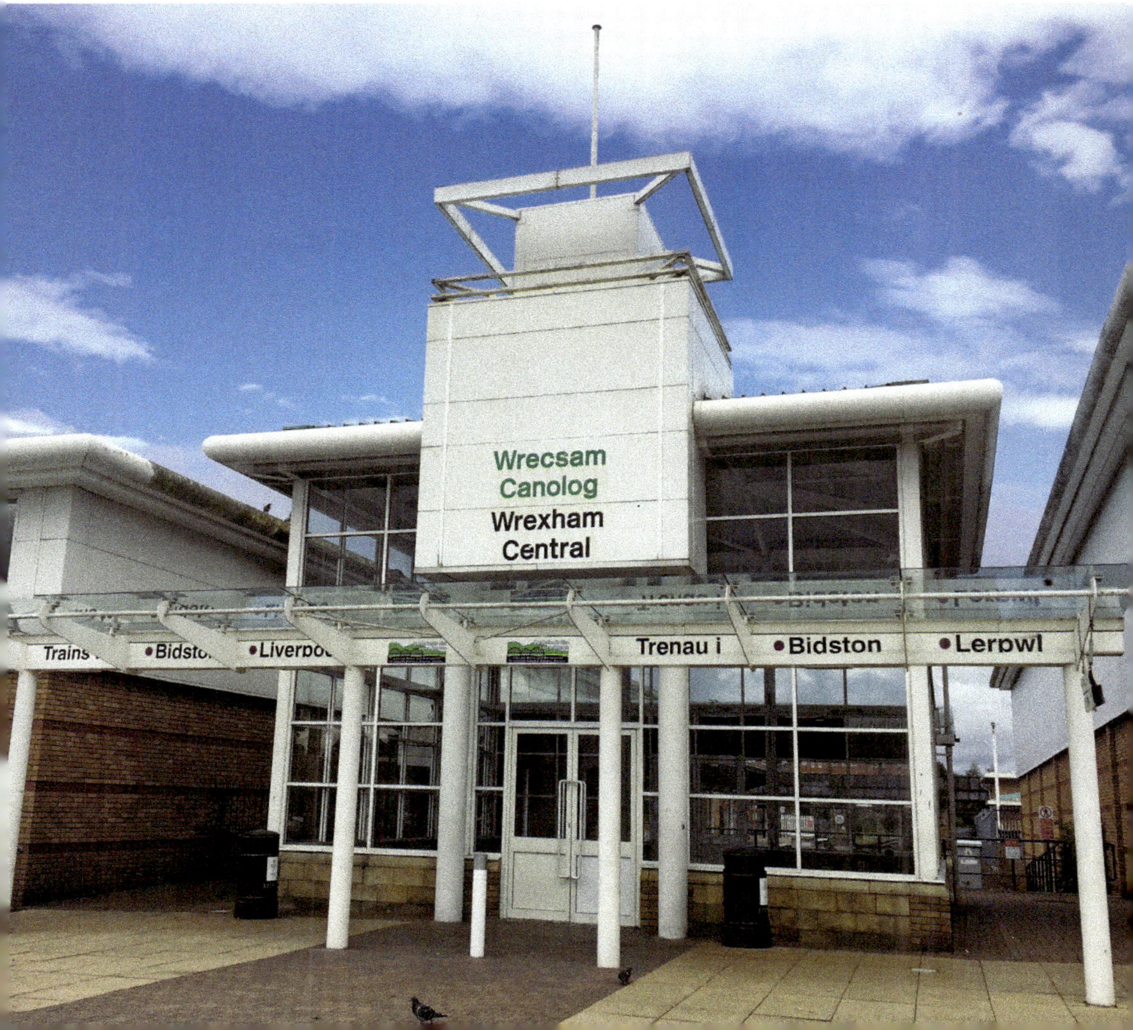

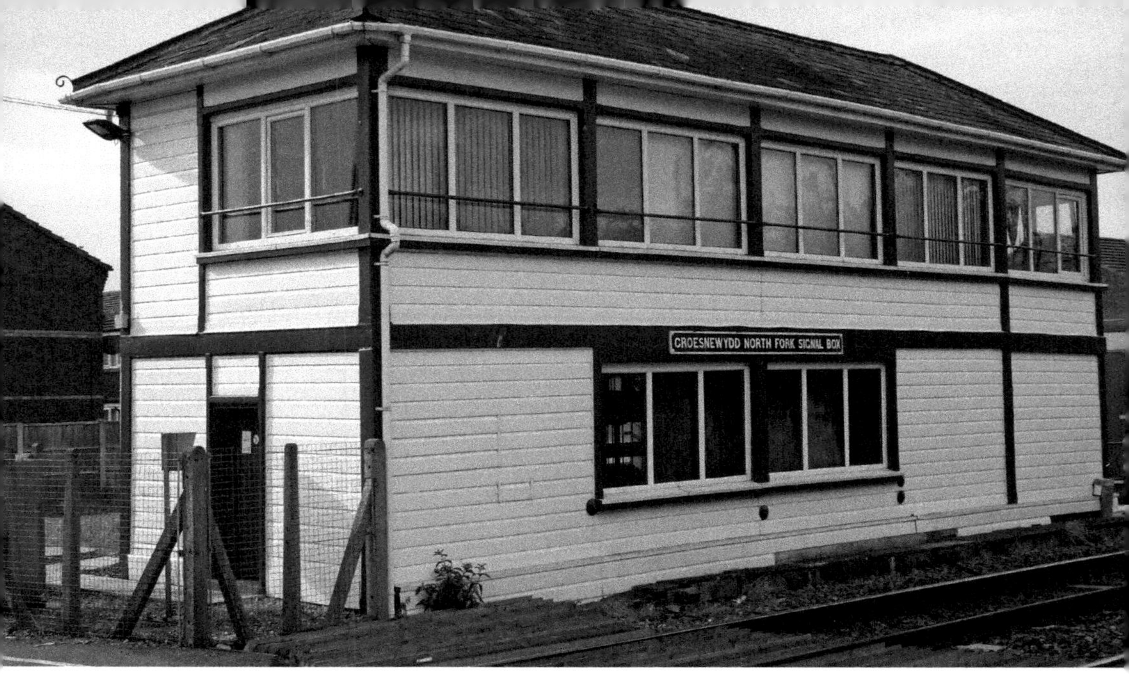

Croes Newydd North Fork signal box stands at the northern end of a triangular junction where the Wrexham and Minera line (now closed) meets the Chester–Shrewsbury line. It was built by the GWR in 1905 to replace a smaller box. Originally of four bays, it was extended on the south possibly to accommodate the eighty-three-lever frame.

Croes Newydd shed was one of two engine sheds in Wrexham, the other being at Rhosddu. Situated on a triangle of land formed by the Ruabon–Wrexham–Brymbo lines, Croes Newydd was built by the GWR in 1902. It was the final 'Northlight' pattern of 'engine shed' to be built by the company. After nationalisation, it became part of the western region of BR and in its final years it came under the control of the LMS region. The shed was closed in June 1967.

RWF Memorial

The Royal Welsh Fusiliers memorial was designed by the Welsh sculptor Sir William Goscombe John RA and commemorates the officers and men of the regiment who were killed in the First World War. It was unveiled in November 1924, and, since then, it has become a memorial to all those of the regiment who have been killed in conflicts since 1914. Originally, the memorial stood at the junction of Grosvenor Road and Regent Street; it was moved to its present position at Bodhyfryd in the 1960s.

The two figures on the memorial represent a fusilier of the eighteenth century passing the colours into the hands of his twentieth-century counterpart. The inscription reads *Pleidiol rwyf i'm Gwlad* (I am loyal to my Country) and *Duw Cadw'r Brenin* (God save the King).

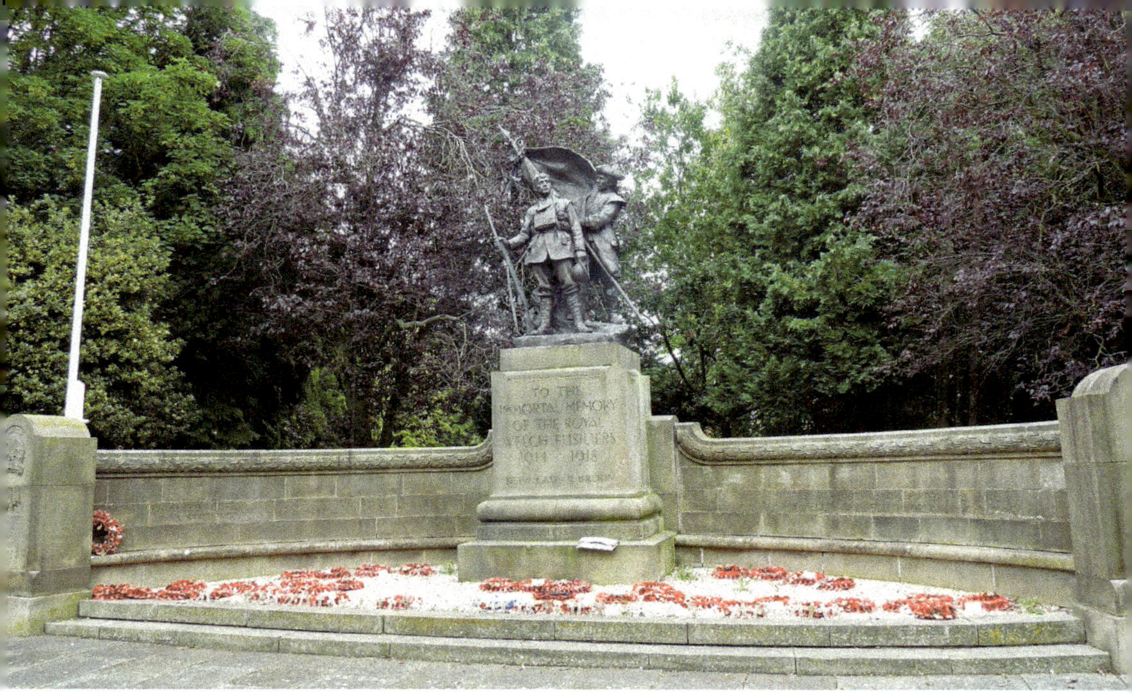

Above: The Royal Welch Fusiliers memorial at Bodhyfryd. Designed by Sir William Goscombe John RA, it was unveiled in 1924 to commemorate those officers and men of the RWF killed in the First World War. The memorial originally stood at the junction of Regent Street and Grosvenor Road before being moved to its present position.

Right: The RWF memorial showing the figure of the eighteenth-century fusilier passing the colours to his twentieth-century counterpart.

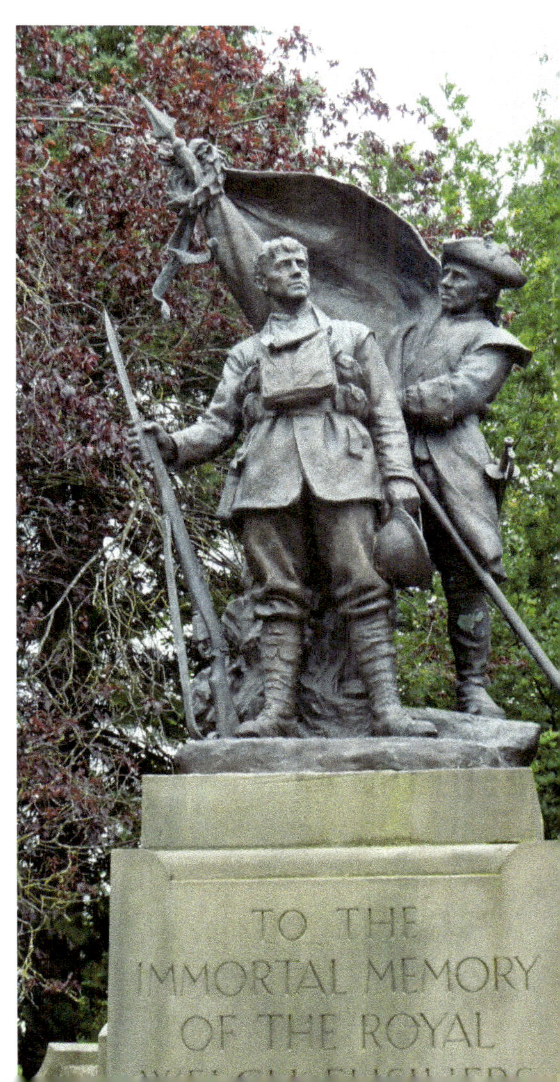

Rivers

The River Clywedog was a key element in the industrial development of Wrexham in the eighteenth and nineteenth centuries. There were some seventeen watermills along this comparatively short river, servicing the cloth, corn, malt and paper mills. The Clywedog rises in the hills west of Minera and meets the River Dee 4 miles south-east of Wrexham. Today, there is a popular 7-mile walking trail which starts at Minera lead mines and finishes at Kings Mills.

The River Gwenfro rises at a number of small springs to the south and east of Bwlchgwyn. The river runs through the centre of Wrexham, where it is largely culverted. It joins the Clywedog at Kings Mills. In the nineteenth century, local children used to catch large eels in the Gwenfro, particularly where the warm water from the lager beer brewery emptied into the river.

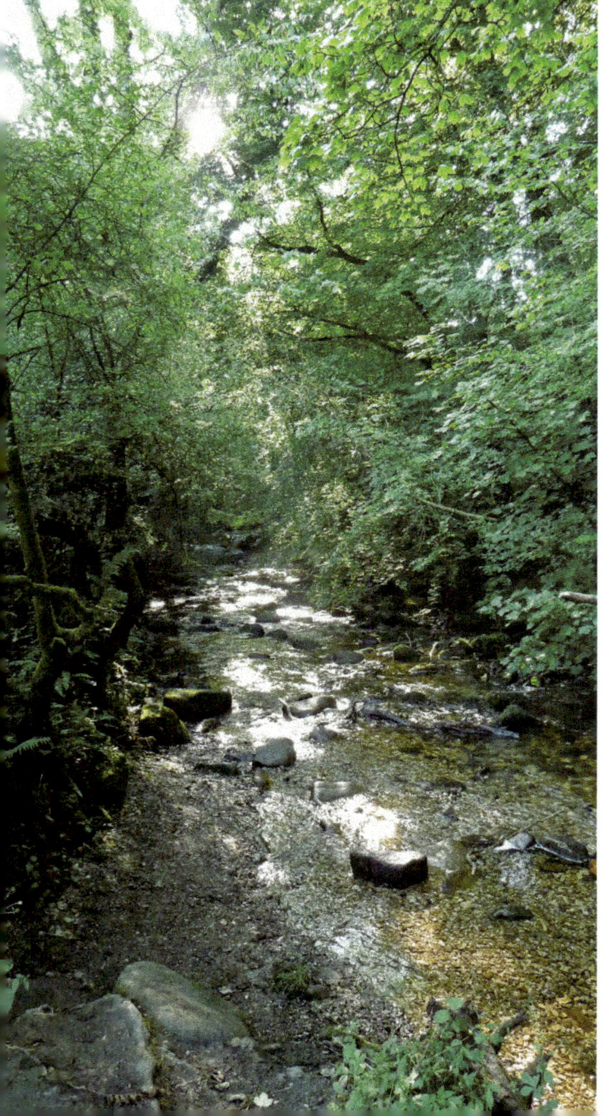

The River Clywedog below Nant Mill. The river was an important source of power in the Clywedog Valley and Wrexham. During the eighteenth and nineteenth centuries there were some seventeen watermills along the river.

Red Brick

Anyone travelling around Wrexham cannot fail to notice the predominance of red brick in buildings of the nineteenth and early twentieth centuries. The discovery of Etruria Marl clay in the Ruabon area in the nineteenth century heralded the beginning of tile, terracotta and brick making on a very large scale. So much so that by the turn of the twentieth century, some 2,000 people were employed in this industry. Ruabon red brick can be found much further afield than Wrexham and, amongst many other buildings, was used for the Pier Head offices in Cardiff and Liverpool university. In fact, the term Redbrick University is said to stem from the use of Ruabon red brick in the building of nineteenth-century universities. Decorative terracotta work is also a feature of many public and commercial buildings in the area. Burton Building in Bridge Street is a good example of a building in red brick with terracotta embellishments.

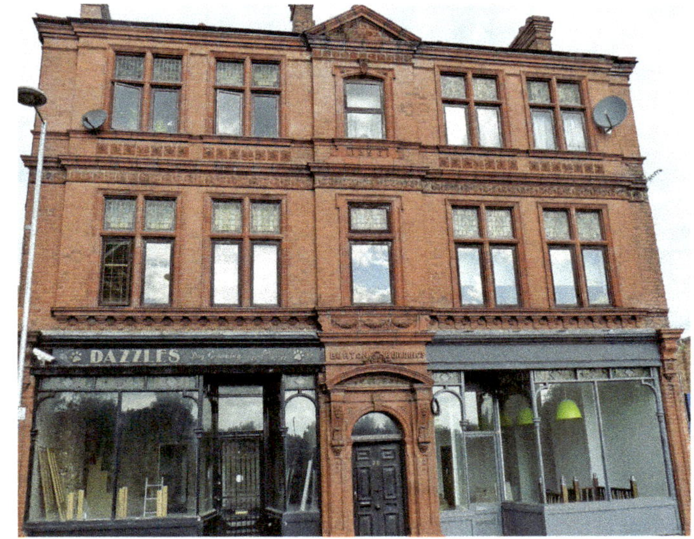

An example of the decorative use of terracotta is the Burton Building, Bridge Street. There are numerous examples of decorative terracotta in and around Wrexham.

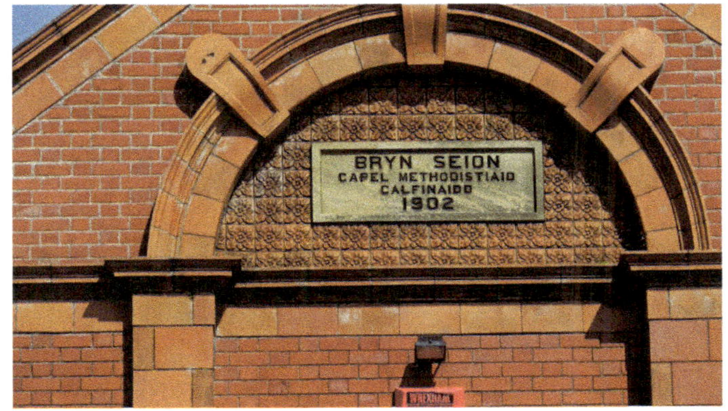

Decorative terracotta work on the front façade of Sion Chapel, Trevor.

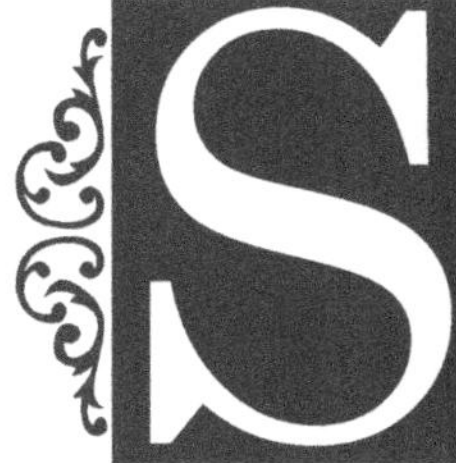

Seven Wonders of Wales

The Seven Wonders of Wales appear in an anonymously written piece of eighteenth-
or early nineteenth-century doggerel. It has been suggested that it was actually written
by an English visitor. If not, it was certainly written by a well-travelled Welshman.
We could also conjecture that it was written before 1805, as it does not mention
Pontcysyllte Aqueduct, which was certainly one of the wonders of the age.

Pistyll Rhaedr and Wrexham steeple
Snowdon's mountain without its people
Overton yew trees, St Winefride's Wells
Llangollen bridge and Gresford bells.

At 240 feet, Pistyll Rhaedr, near Llanrhaeadr-ym-Mochant, is the tallest waterfall
in Wales. Wrexham, of course, does not have a steeple, but St Giles' Church has a
magnificent 130-foot tower. Today, Snowdon is one of the most visited places in North
Wales. For those who have experienced it, the mountain takes on a different dimension
without its many visitors. The churchyard of St Mary the Virgin at Overton-on-Dee
has twenty-one ancient yew trees that are thought to be between 1,500 and 2,000
years old. St Winefride's Well, at Hollywell, Flintshire, lays claim to being the oldest
continually visited pilgrimage site in Britain. It has often been referred to as the
'Lourdes' of Wales. The present Llangollen bridge is actually the third bridge to be
built here. The first being built in the reign of Henry I and the second in around 1345
by John Trevor. The present bridge dates from the sixteenth century and was widened
in 1873 and again in 1968. It is thought that Gresford church bells were included in the
rhyme, as a reflection of their purity of tone.

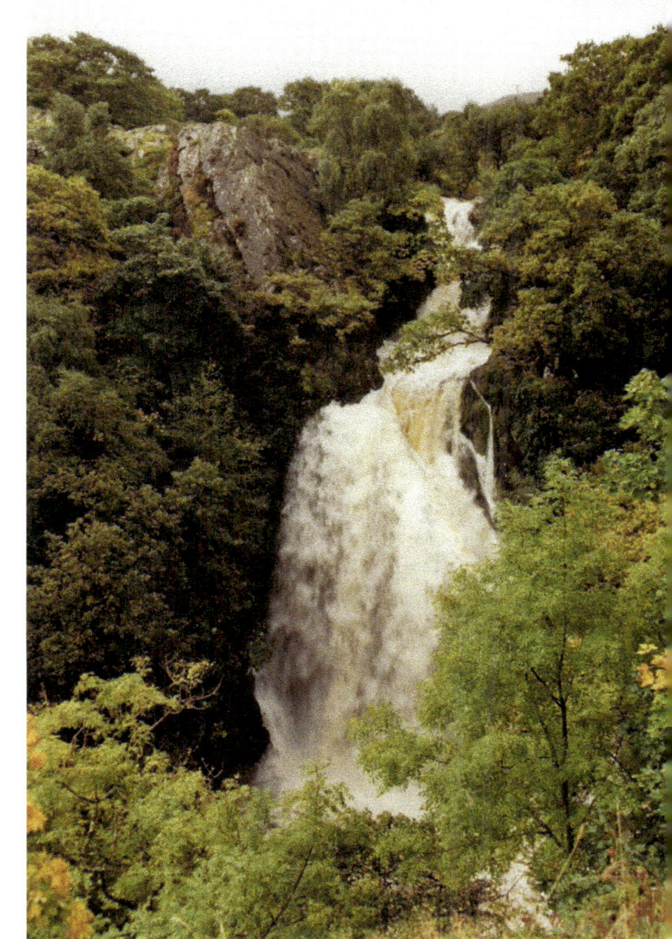

Right: Pistyll Rhaedr near Llanrhaedr-yn-Mochant. At 240 feet this is the tallest waterfall in Wales.

Below: Overton yew trees.

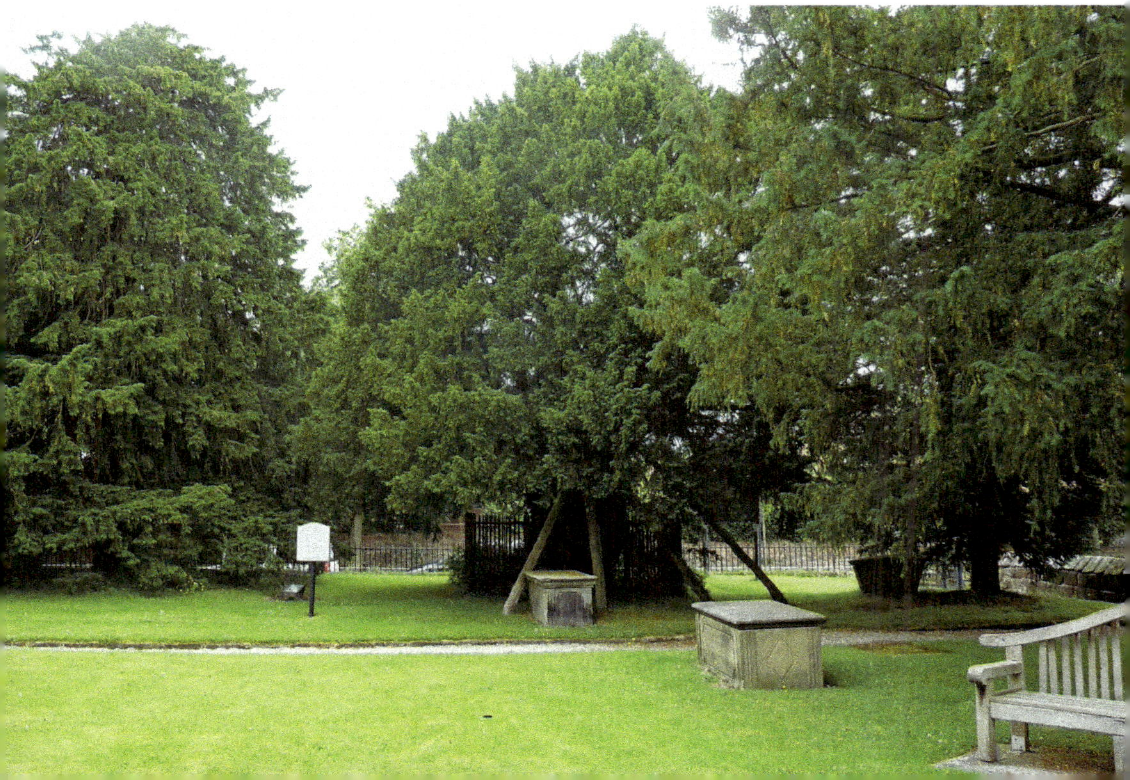

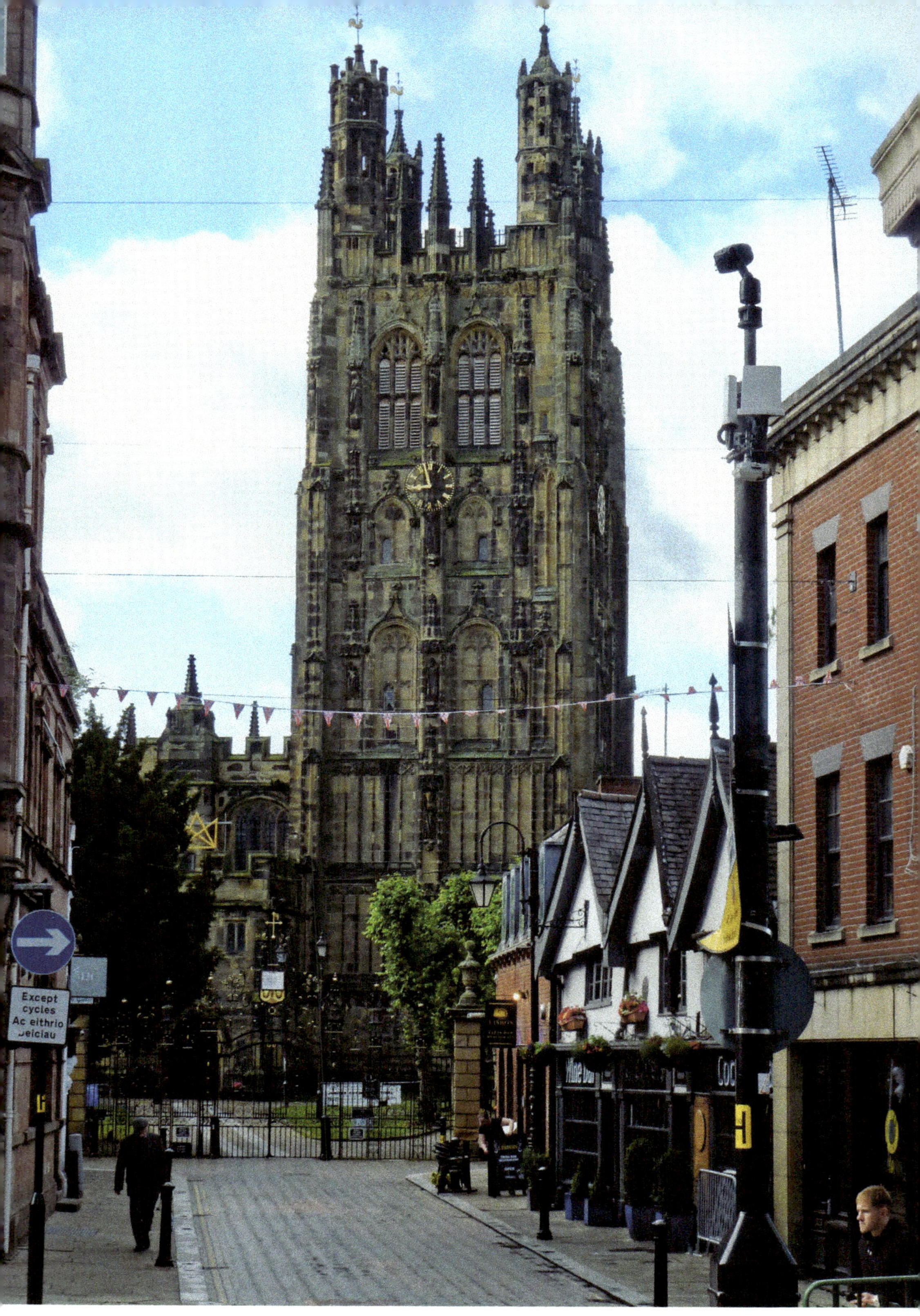

St Giles' Church tower.

In June 2006, the *Western Mail* revealed a list of Wales seven modern wonders as chosen by readers. These were:

The great glasshouses of the National Botanic Gardens of Wales
Mount Snowdon
Wales Millennium Centre
Eisteddfodau
Portmerion
Pontcysyllte Aqueduct
The Pembrokeshire Islands

St Giles' Church

Described by Jenkins as 'The Glory of the Marches' and by Samuel Johnson as 'A very large and magnificent church,' St Giles' is, at 180 feet long, the largest medieval parish church in Wales. Its 136-foot tower dominates the Wrexham skyline. The area in which the church stands was once known as Bryn-y-Grog (Hill of the Cross). The present church was built in the late fifteenth and early sixteenth centuries. Evidence suggests that it is at least the third church on the site. The first written record of a church on this site appears in 1220. The thirteenth-century church was damaged when the steeple was blown down in 1330, after which the church was rebuilt in the Decorated style. The present church was built after its fourteenth-century predecessor was gutted by fire in 1463. The nave arcade retains a fourteenth-century Decorated style and was extensively remodelled in the later fifteenth century. The degree of Tudor symbolism in the church suggests that the work may have been financed by Lady Margaret Beaufort, mother of King Henry VII. The church has a number of interesting monuments including one by the French sculptor Louis-Francois Roubiliac. The north aisle contains stained glass from the studio of Burne-Jones. A rare survival is the Doom painting over the chancel arch.

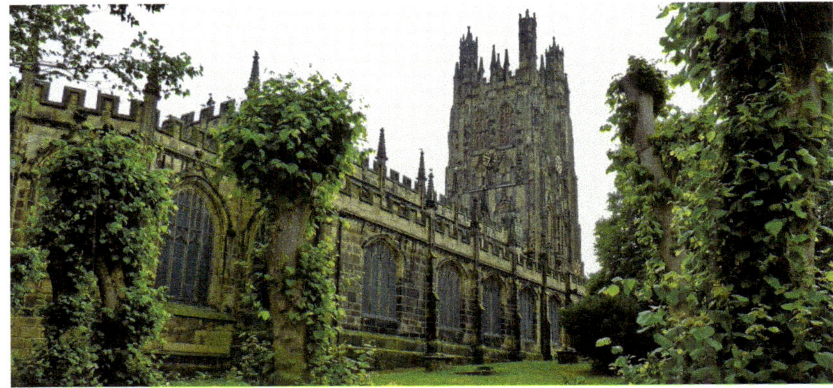

St Giles'
Church.

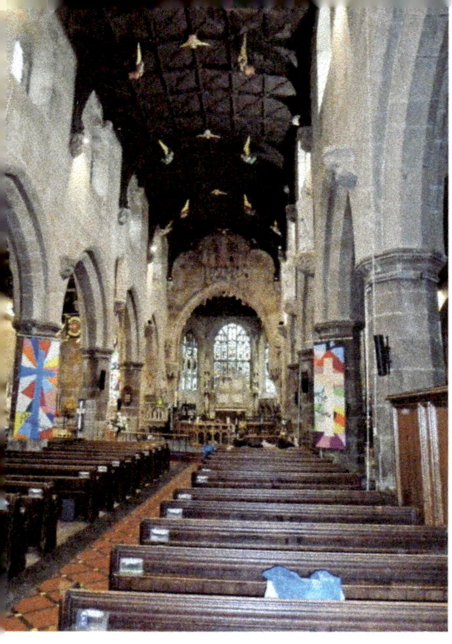

St Giles' Church interior.

St Mary's Roman Catholic Cathedral

St Mary's Roman Catholic Cathedral, or more appropriately the Cathedral Church of Our Lady of Sorrows, was built by local industrialist Richard Thompson in 1857. Designed by Edward Welby Pugin in a fourteenth-century Decorated Gothic style, the cathedral replaced an earlier church in King Street. Built originally as a parish church, it became a pro-cathedral in 1898 when the Roman Catholic Diocese of Menevia was created. The cathedral has a memorial to Richard Gwynn (1535–84), a local Catholic martyr who was executed in Wrexham Beast Market in October 1584; being charged with high treason, his body was hanged, drawn and quartered. Richard Gwynn was beatified by Pope Pius XI in 1929 and he was canonised by Pope Paul VI in 1970.

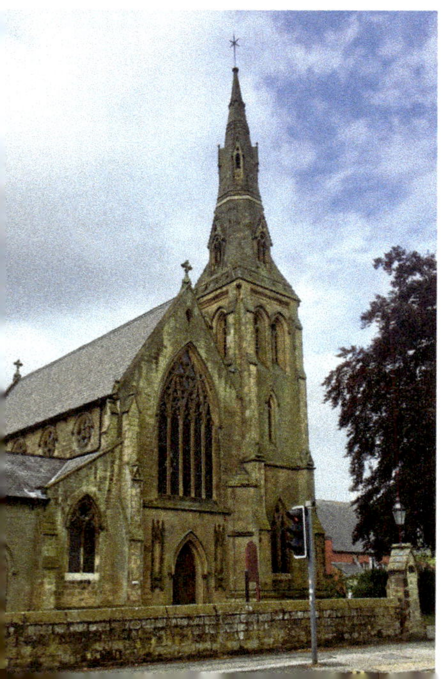

St Mary's Roman Catholic Cathedral, built in 1857 to the design of Edward Welby Pugin. Built originally as a parish church, it became a pro-cathedral in 1898 when the Roman Catholic Diocese of Geneva was created.

Trevor Hall

Trevor Hall (originally known as Llys Trefor) sits at the very edge of Wrexham County Borough, but as one of the very few Georgian houses in the area, it deserves to be included. The site, which overlooks the Dee Valley, is an ancient one and it is known that Bishop Trevor, who built the original Llangollen bridge in 1345, lived here. The present house was built by John Lloyd of Glanhavon, Montgomeryshire, who married Mary Trevor (heiress of the Trevor estates) in 1715. The design of the house and the actual building of it are attributed to John Roberts, and this is reflected on a stone on the outside of the house which bears the initials of John and Mary Lloyd, the date 1742 and the name John Roberts. It also bears the Latin motto *Dum Spiro Spero* ('While I breath I Hope').

By the early part of the nineteenth century, the house had left the Lloyd family when the last heiress married Rice Thomas of Coed Helen, near Caernarfon. Rice Thomas extended the house by adding one bay on the west in order to create a spacious dining room and a drawing room above. The Thomas family owned the hall until after the Second World War, but it ceased to be their home after they moved away sometime in 1820. During the nineteenth century the hall was leased to various tenants, the most notable of which were the Edwards family, proprietors of the Trefynant Fireclay Works of Ruabon. Three generations of the family lived at Trevor Hall before they surrendered the lease in 1956, when the hall reverted to the Coed Helen estate.

The hall was then purchased by a local timber merchant, who applied to demolish the house in order to build four houses on the site. This was strongly opposed by local groups and, following a public enquiry in 1961, a preservation order was put on the hall. It was acquired by the WRVS in 1963, with the intention of turning it into a children's home. However, a major fire reduced the house to a shell and it was purchased by a local farmer, who installed a temporary roof to provide shelter for his livestock.

In 1987, the hall was purchased by Michael Tree, who began the long work of restoring the property. In 1998, the work was completed and the hall again put on the market, when it was acquired by Louis Parker and following his death in 1999, it reverted to his widow Mrs L. Parker. Today, the Grade I listed hall can be hired for weddings and other special events.

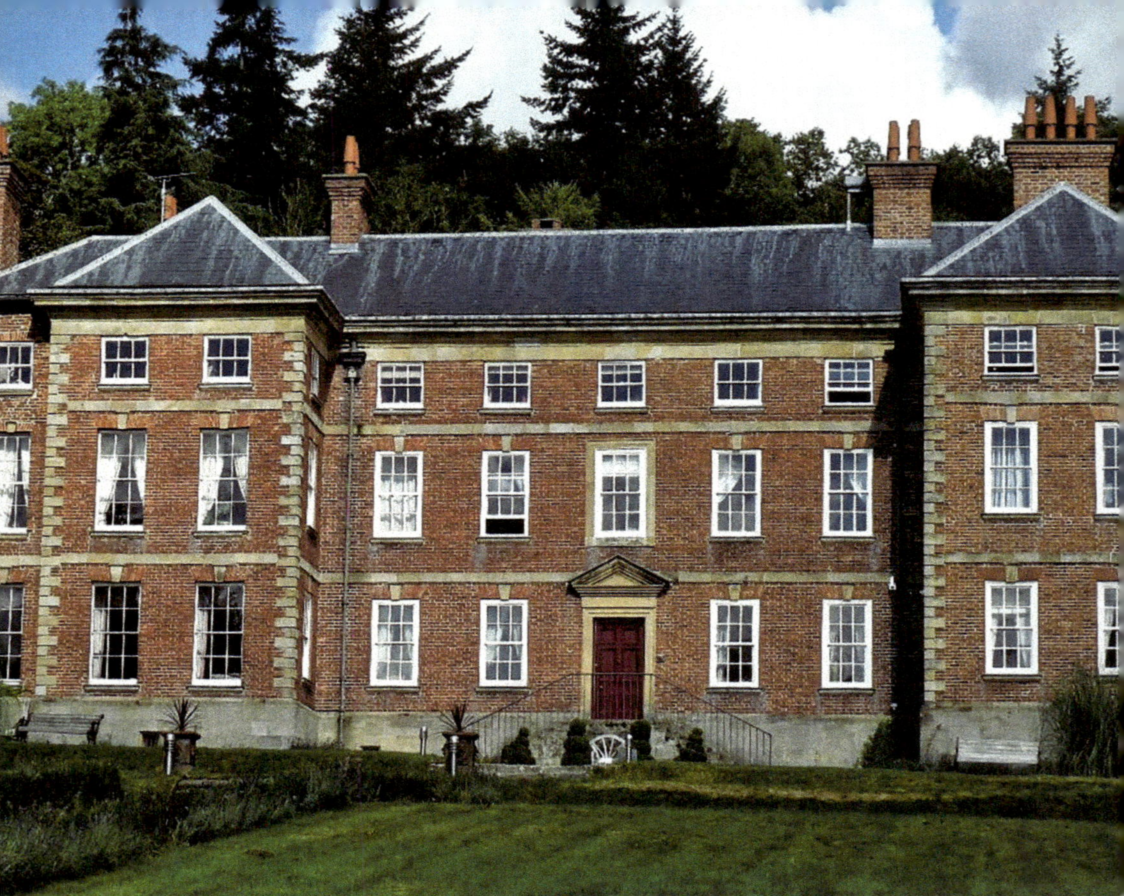

Trevor Hall. This fine Georgian hall replaced an earlier building on the site and was built by John and Mary Lloyd in 1742.

Trevor Church

Trevor Church lies just a few yards from the hall, hidden in the trees. The church was consecrated in 1772, but was built earlier in the eighteenth century as a private chapel for the Lloyds of Trevor Hall. It is almost certain that there was an earlier church on this site. The earliest date suggested for the present building is 1717, although 1742 has also been suggested. Internally, the church is a single cell structure, with a small vestry added in the nineteenth century. Later traceried windows are likely to date from 1841, when refurnishing took place. The pulpit looks Jacobean, but is possibly made up from fragments. The church has nineteenth-century box pews with hat pegs above them.

The east window has twentieth-century stained glass by the famed Chester glass artist Trena Cox. There are fragments of medieval glass in two of the windows, which is thought to have come from Valle Crucis Abbey. There is a two-tiered chandelier with dove and wrought-iron suspension.

Although built originally for the family at Trevor Hall, today the church is part of the Llangollen group of churches, and serves the communities of Garth and Trevor.

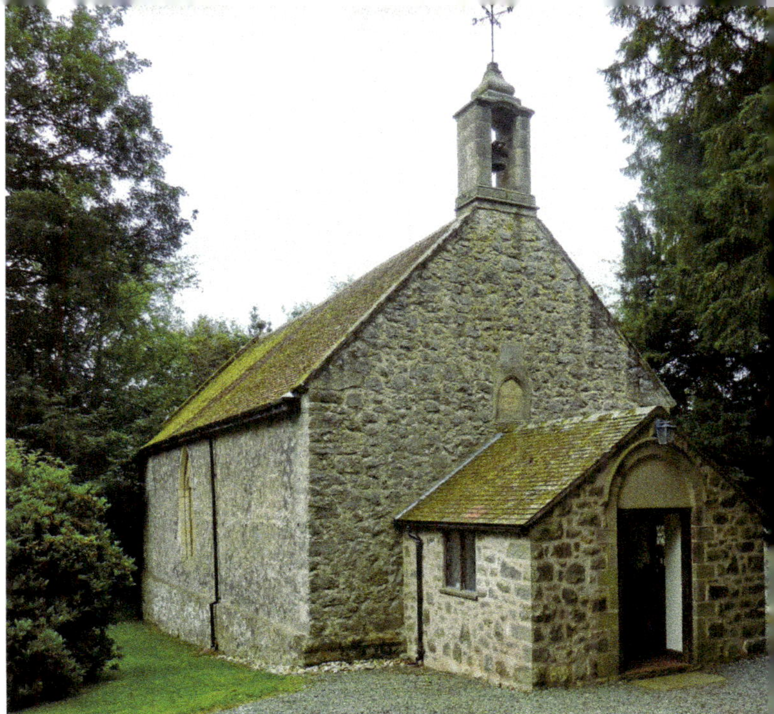

Trevor Church. Nestled in the trees below Trevor Hall, the church was built by John Lloyd as the family chapel.

Trevor Basin

The area that is now Trevor Basin was used originally to store and prepare materials for the building of the aqueduct. By the time the aqueduct was completed, the decision not to carry the canal forward to Chester had already been made, so the basin was created to transship local goods from horse-drawn tramways to the canal.

Situated on the basin, and mostly ignored by visitors heading for the aqueduct, are two of the three most important bridges on the Llangollen Canal. The first, Rhos-y-coed bridge, is situated where the canal branches off to Llangollen; the second, Scotch Hall bridge, is the three arched bridge which carries New Road over the canal. Both of these bridges demonstrate the earliest use of cast iron anywhere on the system, using cambered cast iron girders to support ashlar stone to form a flattened arch. Both bridges were designed by Telford and bridge 29 is unique in being the only three-arched bridge of its type still in its original position.

In the short arm of the canal, which was originally intended to take it to Ruabon, a stone loading pier was constructed that divides the canal into two arms. Here goods were transshipped from tramways to the canal boats. At the end of the eastern arm the point at which the Plas Kynaston Canal branched off can be seen. The Plan Kynaston Canal was constructed in sections during the 1820s and 1830s by Exuperius Pickering and Thomas Edward Ward to serve the coal, lime and iron making industries in Cefn Mawr. The branch was authorised in 1820, and was originally intended to reach as far as Plas Kynaston Hall. However, it only ever reached the rear of the Queens Head Hotel.

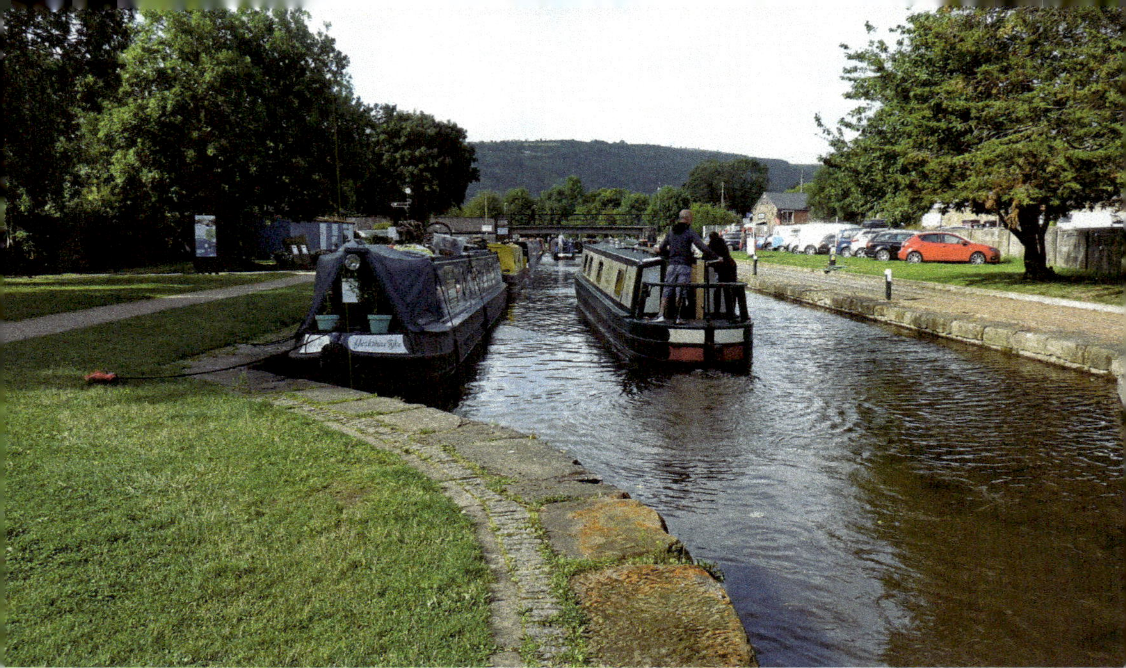

Trevor Basin. Once busy with the transport of coal, iron, limestone, slate, tiles and bricks by canal, today the basin has adapted to meet the needs of the leisure industry and is particularly busy in the summer months with canal hire boats, canoeists, paddle boarders and fishermen. In addition, many thousands of people visit each year to see Pontcysyllte Aqueduct.

Today, the basin, like the rest of the canal network in Wales and England, is under the care of the Canal and River Trust. It is a busy centre for the hire of canal boats and boat trips across the aqueduct. Many thousands of visitors come from all over the world to view the Pontcysyllte Aqueduct. The visitor centre contains a wide range of information about the aqueduct and the surrounding area.

Thomas Telford

Travelling through North Wales, it is not difficult to see the evidence of the work done by Telford almost 200 years ago. Canals apart, in his lifetime Telford was responsible for over 1,000 bridges and some 900 miles of road, which included the A5 that connects London with Holyhead. This was one of the major civil engineering achievements of the age and included the iron Waterloo bridge at Betws-y-Coed and the Menai suspension bridge across the Menai Strait to Anglesey. Telford was ever a man for detail and concerned himself with the smaller details as well as great bridges. The milestones along the Holyhead road and houses for the tollkeepers were all designed by him. Born in Scotland in 1757, Thomas Telford was originally apprenticed to a stonemason. Following periods of work in Edinburgh, London and Portsmouth, he moved to Shrewsbury where he practiced as a self-taught architect. In 1787, he secured the post of County Surveyor for Shropshire, with responsibility for the county's public buildings and bridges. His reputation in Shropshire was such that, six years later, in 1793, he was appointed as agent and engineer to the Ellesmere

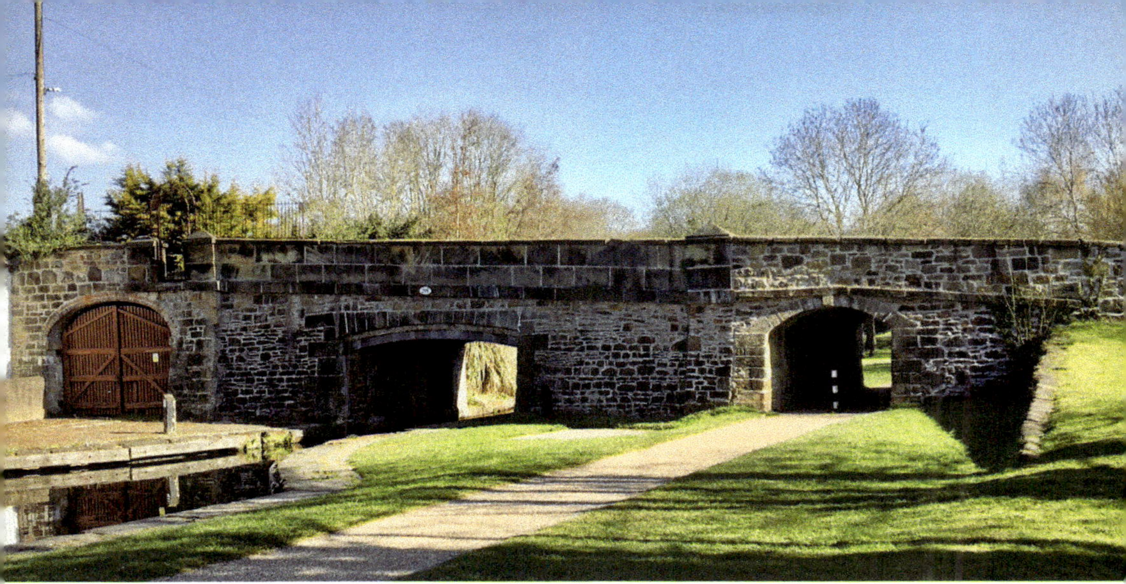

Scotch Hall Bridge, with its flanking arches for horse-drawn tramways. This bridge, and Rhos-y-Coed bridge, are important for use of cast-iron beams to strengthen the masonry. Scotch Hall Bridge is possibly the only bridge of its type still in its original position.

Canal. In this role he worked with William Jessop and was quick to develop his knowledge of both waterways and the use of iron in construction. He was responsible for the iron bridge across the River Severn at Buildwas and for the use of iron in the construction of the aqueduct at Longdon on Tern. Having learned much about canals from Jessop, Telford went on to design a number of other canals including the Caledonian Canal, the Birmingham canal line and the Birmingham and Liverpool Junction Canal. He also advised on the building of the 118-mile-long Göta Canal in Sweden. Jacob Bronowski, writing in *The Ascent of Man*, in describing Telford said 'His greatest aqueduct that carries the Llangollen Canal over the River Dee shows him to have been a master of cast iron on the grand scale.' Thomas Telford died in 1834 and was buried in the nave of Westminster Abbey.

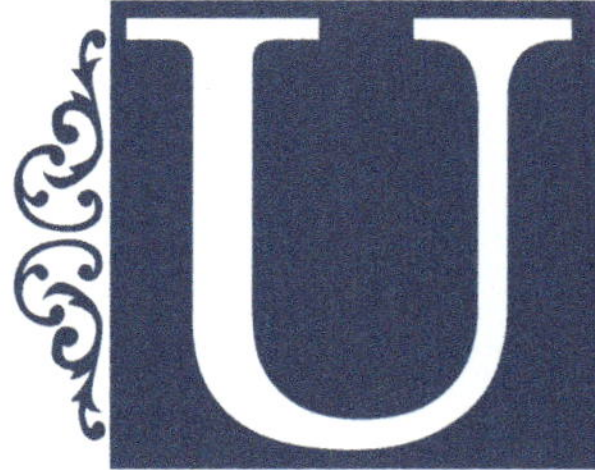

University

The origins of Wrexham Glyndwr University can be traced back to the Wrexham School of Science and Art (WSSA) in 1887. The WSSA began offering degrees in science validated by the University of London in 1924. In succeeding years, there were a number of name changes, becoming the Denbighshire Technical Institute in 1927 and the Denbighshire Technical College in 1939. In 1975, the name changed again to the North East Wales Institute of Higher Education, with degrees, initially validated by Salford University. In 1993, the college became associate members of the University of Wales, before becoming full members in 2004. In 2008, the university received full accreditation and was able to deliver its own degrees. At the same time, the institute was renamed Glyndwr University. However, in 2016, this was changed to Wrexham Glyndwr University.

The university has two sites in Wrexham: the main Plas Coch campus and the North Wales School of Art and Design in Regent Street. The William Aston Concert Hall is also part of the Plas Coch campus.

Wrexham Glyndwr University. Tracing its origins back to 1887, the university became full members of the University of Wales in 2004.

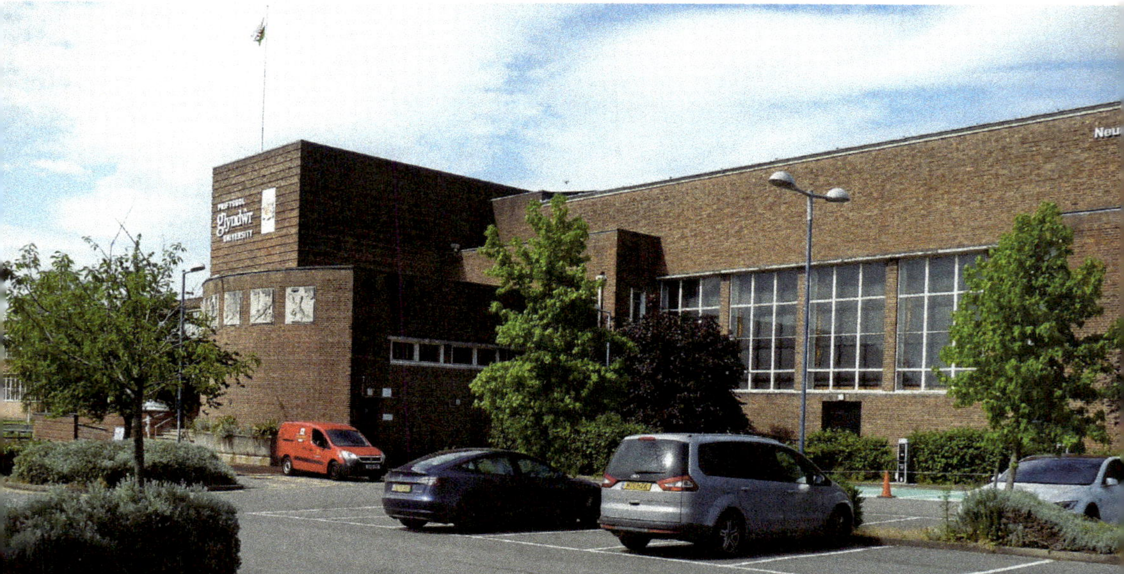

Union Vaults, Yorke Street

The use of terracotta as an architectural embellishment is quite common in Wrexham and the surrounding area. Its use varies from small panels to quite complex frontages as is the case with the Union Vaults. In 1905, the frontage of the building was moved back to facilitate the realignment of Yorke Street and Mount Street. This work afforded the owners the opportunity to create an interesting terracotta frontage which incorporated the name of the brewery, as well as that of the pub. Today, it is no longer a pub, but has been taken over as an Indian restaurant.

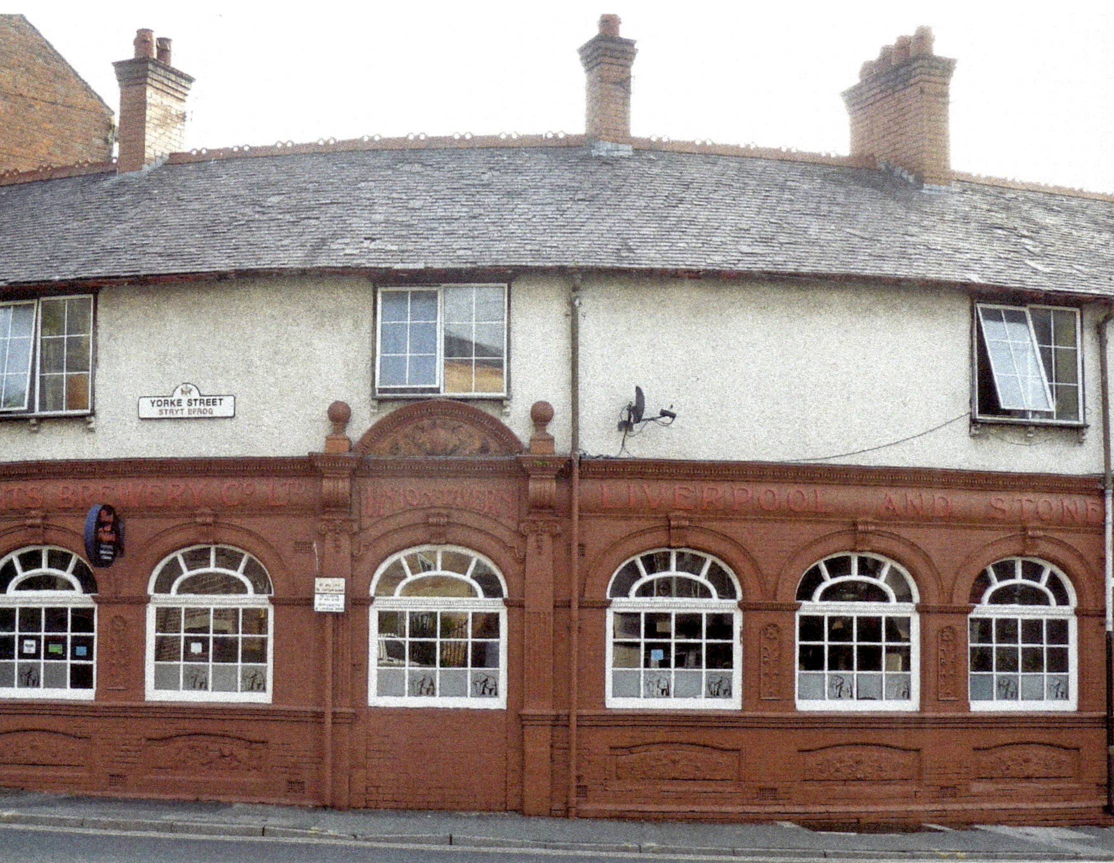

The former Union Vaults, Yorke Street. A good example of the use of terracotta as an architectural embellishment dating from 1905.

Viaducts

Cefn Mawr Viaduct was designed by Henry Robertson, Chief Engineer of the Chester–Shrewsbury Railway, and built by Thomas Brassey. It was built of Cefn sandstone from the (now disused) Chathams Quarry and took some two years to complete at a cost of £72,346. Standing some 147 feet above the river, the viaduct carries the Chester–Shrewsbury Railway line across the Dee Valley and was opened in October 1848. As was often the case in those distant days, the viaduct was opened amid great ceremony with the first train across carrying many local dignitaries. Unfortunately, the train broke down halfway across, and was stranded on the viaduct overnight. The work of Thomas Brassey is synonymous with railways. Born at Buerton, Cheshire, in 1805, he is credited with being responsible for something like a third of Britain's railways up to 1847. It has also been claimed that by his death in 1870, he had built one in every 20 miles of railway in the world.

Chirk Viaduct carries the Chester–Shrewsbury Railway across the Ceiriog Valley. This viaduct was also designed by Henry Robertson and built by Thomas Brassey. It was completed in 1848 and rebuilt in 1858. The viaduct is 849 feet long with sixteen arches, ten of which form the major span. It stands some 100 feet high and 30 feet above the adjacent canal aqueduct.

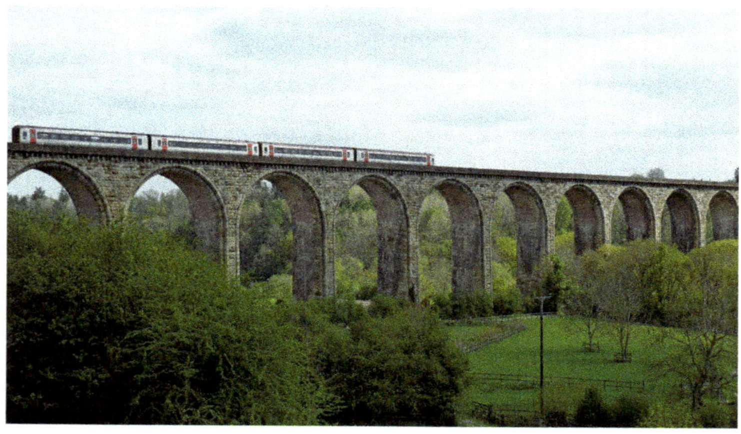

Cefn Mawr railway viaduct was built by Thomas Brassey in 1848 to carry the Chester–Shrewsbury line over the Dee Valley.

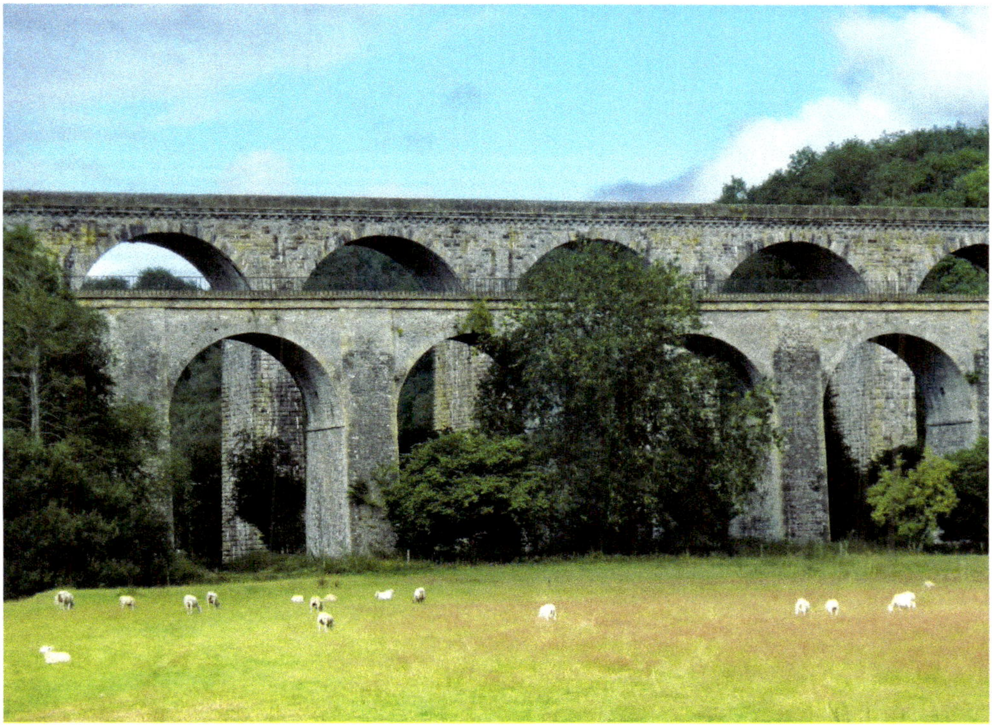

Above: Chirk railway viaduct. This viaduct was also built by Thomas Brassey and carries the Chester–Shrewsbury line over the Ceiriog Valley. Standing some 30 feet above the adjacent aqueduct, the viaduct is 849 feet long and is carried on ten 45-foot arches, with another three arches at either end to replace an earlier wooden arch at either end.

Right: The bust of Thomas Brassey in Chester Cathedral.

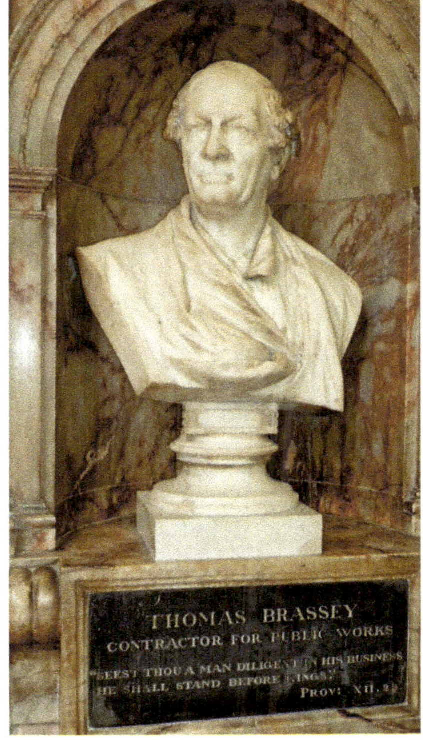

Valle Crucis Abbey

Although Valle Crucis Abbey is outside of the Wrexham County Borough area, its connections with Wrexham are sufficient to merit its inclusion here. This Cistercian abbey lies at the foot of the Horseshoe Pass, just a few miles outside Llangollen. Valle Crucis was founded in 1201 by Madog ap Gruffudd Maelor, who was the ruler of northern Powys. The abbey was initially colonised by monks from Strata Marcella. On its completion, the abbey community was thought to be about sixty, twenty choir monks and forty lay members. During the medieval period, the abbey was known as Abbatia de Llangwest, from the original Welsh name for the site, Llanegwestl. The Latin name Valle Crucis (Valley of the Cross) is derived from the nearby Pillar of Eliseg, a ninth-century memorial cross set up by Cyngen ap Cadell, king of Powis, in honour of his great grandfather Elisedd ap Gwylog.

The abbey suffered during the wars of Edward I and in the uprising of Owain Glyndwr, and it was closed by Henry VIII in 1537 as part of the Dissolution of the Monasteries. The abbey appears to have been struggling in its final year, and John Durham, the last abbot, was known to have been borrowing heavily in order to keep the abbey running. After its closure, the abbey fell into serious disrepair. However,

Valle Crucis Abbey, founded in 1201 by Madog ap Gruffudd. This photograph shows the east end of the abbey, with the only surviving monastic fishpond in the foreground.

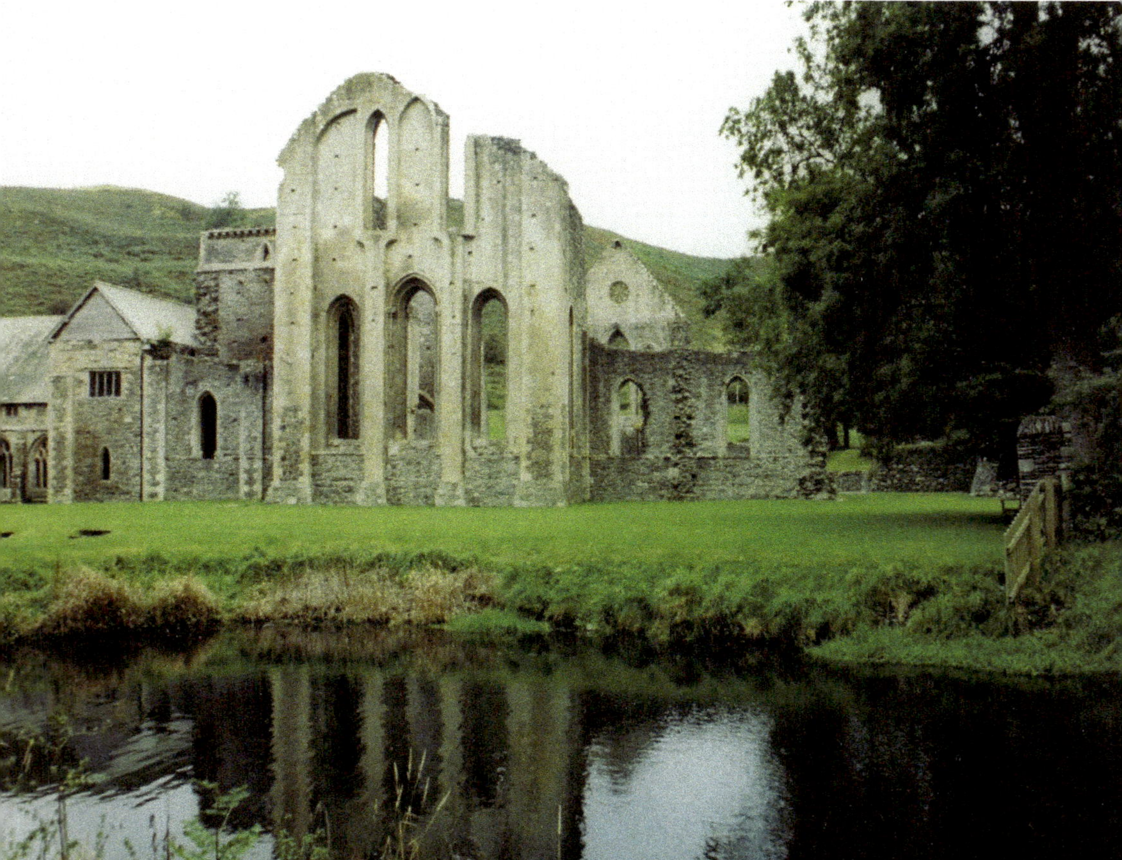

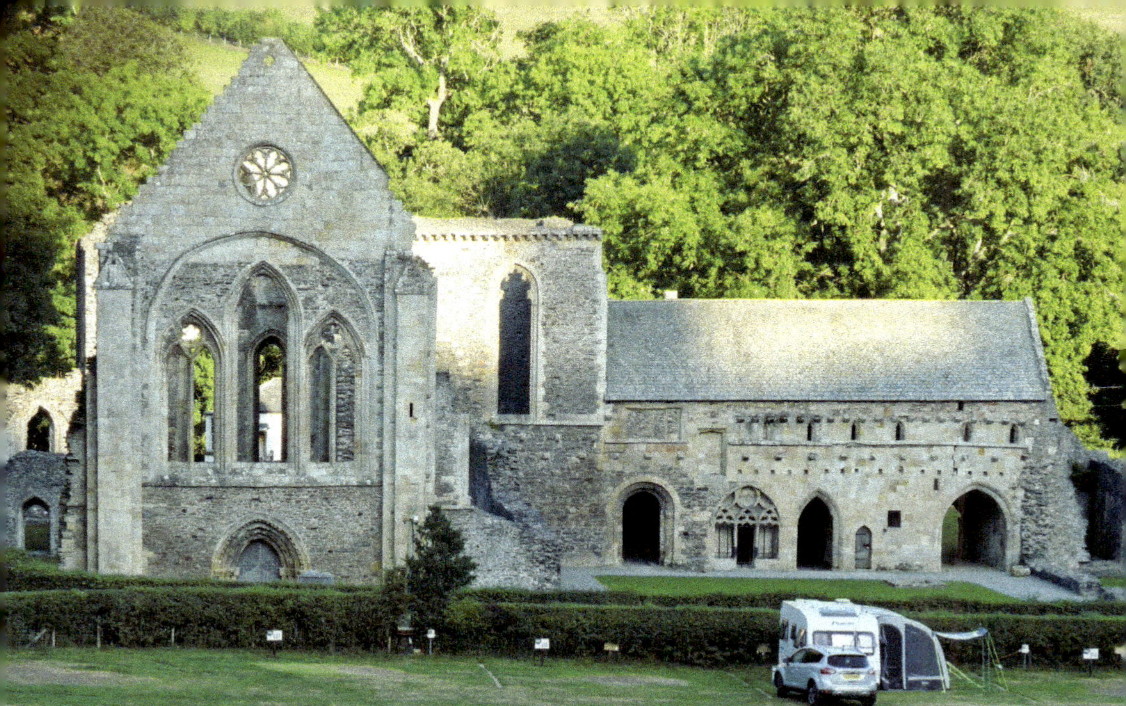

Valle Crucis Abbey. The west front of the abbey with its rose window.

large parts of the structure still survive, including its striking west front with its rose
window; still visible is the inscription 'Adam Abbas Fecit hoc opus in pace quiescat.'
Valle Crucis also has the only surviving monastic fishpond in Wales. The abbey is now
in the care of CADW.

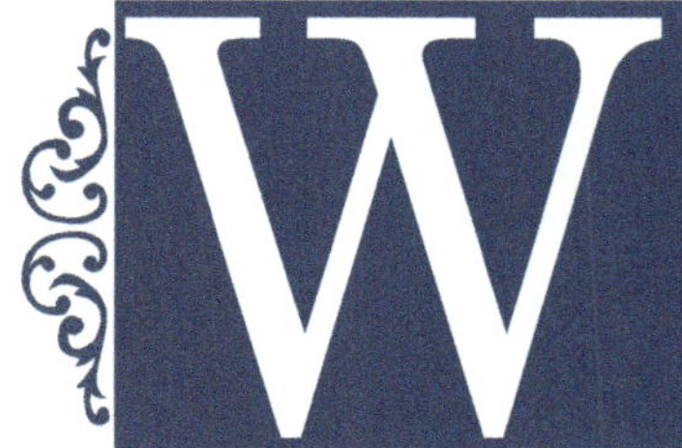

Wynnstay Hall

Wynnstay Hall is around 1.3 km south-east of Ruabon. Originally called Watstay, the name was changed to Wynnstay when the property was inherited in the seventeenth century by Sir John Wynn, through his marriage to Jane Evans, daughter of Eyton Evans of Watstay. The hall appears to have developed from a seventeenth-century timber-framed house, and underwent a number of changes in succeeding years. It was enlarged and remodelled by Francis Smith between 1726 and 1728 and the building was recased in the early nineteenth century, possibly by Benjamin Gunmow. The gardens were laid out by Capability Brown between 1774 and 1784. Princess Victoria is known to have stayed at the house with her mother the Duchess of Kent.

During a period of building work in 1858, the house was severely damaged by fire, leaving only the stone tower and the service areas untouched. Following the fire, the house was rebuilt by Benjamin Ferry in a sixteenth-century French Renaissance style. Writing in the *Wynns at Wynnstay*, T. W. Pritchard opined that the house had 'been transformed from a light elegant Georgian mansion to a gloomy chateau.' During the Second World War, the Royal Engineers Survey Department were based at Wynnstay Hall.

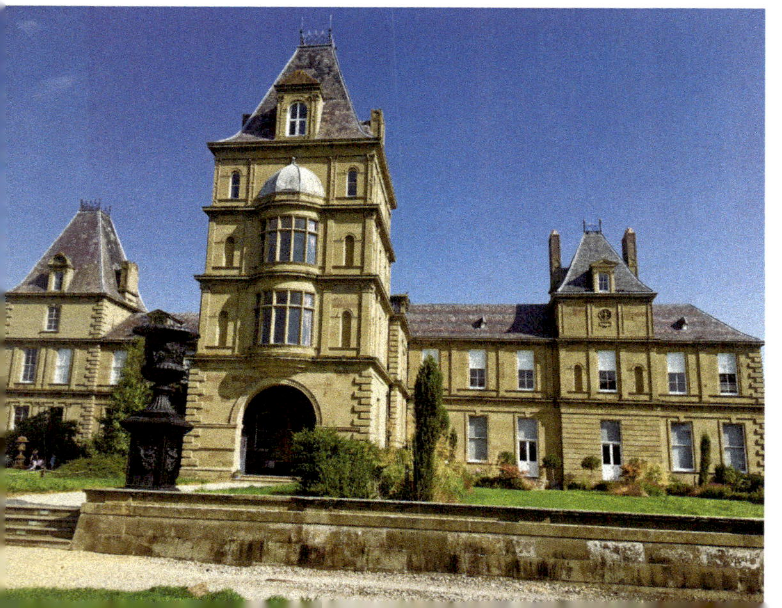

Wynnstay Hall. Once the home of the Williams-Wynn family, the hall was rebuilt in the mid-nineteenth century following a disastrous fire.

In the mid-twentieth century, the Williams-Wynn family vacated the property and moved to nearby Plas Belan. In 1950, the house was purchased by Lindisfarne College and for the next forty-four years was a private boarding school. However, in 1994, the school closed due to financial difficulties. The house has since been turned into prestigious flats and houses.

Wynnstay Arms Hotel

This large hotel in Yorke Street began in the early eighteenth century as a small inn called The George. By the mid-eighteenth century, the inn had been enlarged and renamed The Eagles. The name change probably reflects the fact that the inn was owned by the Williams Wynn family, who featured spread eagles as part of their coat of arms. By the 1830s the inn was known as the Wynnstay Arms. During the 1960s, it was proposed to demolish the building. However, in view of public pressure, the outer wall facing High Street and Yorke Street was retained, while the rest of the building was demolished and a new, more modern hotel built behind it. The original coaching entrance facing Yorke Street was converted into the hotel's main entrance. The Football Association of Wales was formed here.

Wynnstay Arms Hotel, Wrexham, is an early eighteenth-century inn that has changed its name on a number of occasions. Due to public pressure, the eighteenth-century frontage was retained when the hotel was modernised in the 1960s.

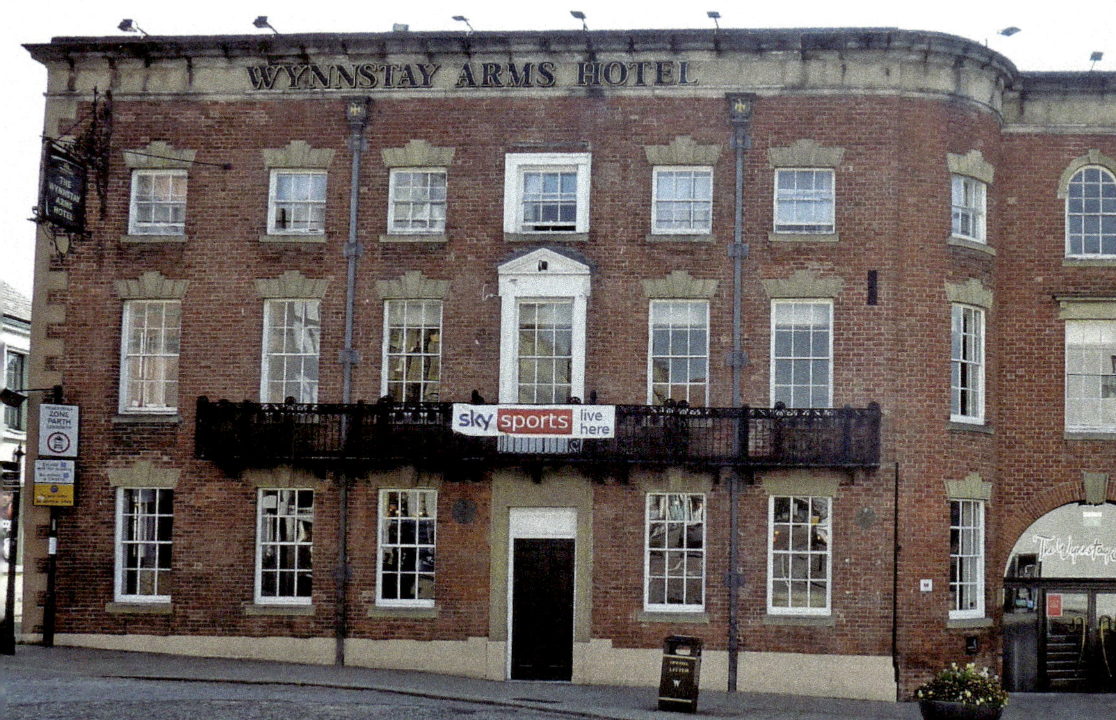

World Heritage Site

UNESCO made the 11 miles of canal from Horseshoe Falls to Chirk Bank a World Heritage Site in July 2009. The UNESCO citation states 'The Pontcysyllte Aqueduct is a pioneering masterpiece of engineering and monumental architecture.' It continues by saying, 'The Pontcysyllte Aqueduct and canal are early and outstanding examples of the innovations brought about by the Industrial Revolution in Britain, where they made decisive development in transport capacities possible. They bear witness to very substantial international interchanges and influences in the fields of inland waterways, civil engineering, and-use planning and the application of iron in structural design.' This designation by UNESCO reflects the historical importance of the Pontcysyllte Aqueduct and ranks it alongside such important buildings as Westminster Abbey and the Tower of London.

Wrexham Place Name

Hywel Wyn Owen and Richard Morgan, writing in the *Dictionary of the Place Names of Wales*, suggest that the name originates from the water-meadow of Wryhtel. The rivers Gwenfro and Clywedog formed the water-meadows associated with Wryhtel, who remains unidentified. In the medieval period there are various spellings of the name. Thus we have Wristlesha in 1161, Wrexham in 1200 and Gwrexam in 1254. Although there are other variations over the centuries, Gwrexam appears again in 1560 and Gwrexham in 1700.

Xplore

Xplore Science Discovery Centre is now located in Henblas Street, in Wrexham town centre. The educational charity North Wales Science opened the original centre on the Wrexham Glyndwr University Plus Coch site in 2003. In partnership with Techniquest it was known as Techniquest Glyndwr. In 2019, the charity moved to its present premises in Henblas Street, and is now known as Xplore Science Discovery Centre. The centre is open to schools and the general public and has over sixty-five hands-on exhibits.

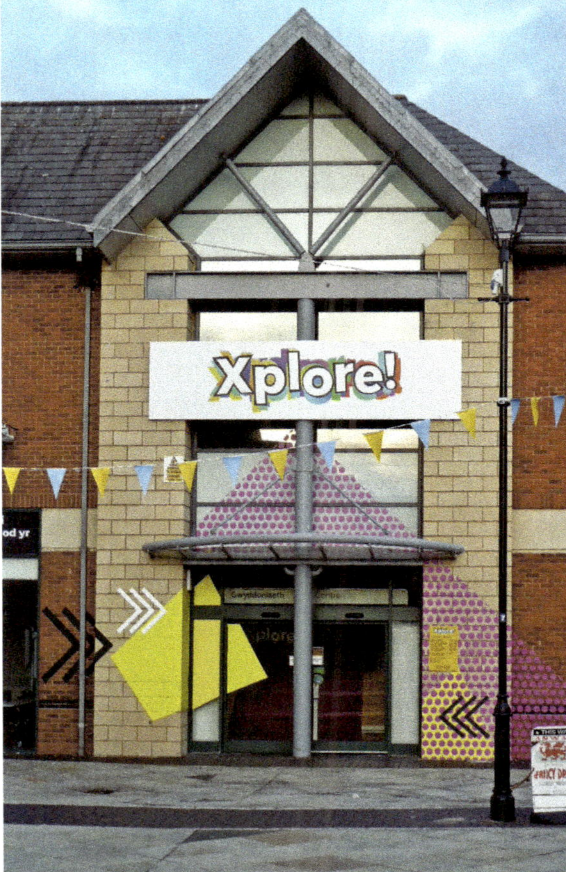

Xplore. This science discovery centre was, for many years, based on the Glyndwr University campus. It moved to Henblas Street in 2020.

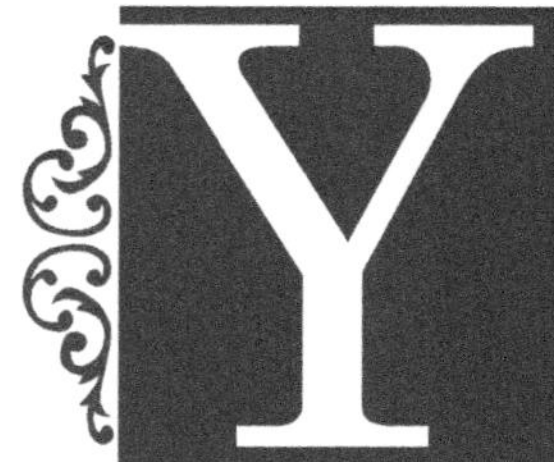

Yale, Elihu

Elihu Yale was born in Boston, Massachusetts, on 5 April 1649. However, his family returned to England when Elihu was three years old and he was educated privately in London. When he left school he initially worked with his father before joining the Honourable East India Company as a clerk. He travelled to India in 1671 and over the next sixteen years worked his way up to become Governor of Fort St George, Madras. In 1692, he was charged by the East India Company of 'self aggrandisement at the company's expense.' In other words, he was indulging in private trade. He was forced to stay in India until 1699, when he returned to England, having, one way or another, made a sizeable fortune during his time in India.

He become involved in the diamond trade for a while, and spent his time between London and Plas Grono. The family connection with Wrexham had begun in the sixteenth century, when Elihu's grandfather bought the Plas Grono estate. Yale's association with the American university that eventually bore his name is well known. In 1718, Cotton Mather, who represented the Collegiate School of Connecticut, wrote to Yale asking for his help in raising funds for a new building. Yale sent him 417 books, a portrait of King George I and nine bales of goods. The college sold these for £800 and, in gratitude, named the new building Yale. Eventually, the whole institution became known as Yale University. Controversial in his own time, Yale still attracts controversy. One of his responsibilities as president of Fort George was oversight of its slave trade. Although Yales himself was never a slave trader, he did not own slaves and, in fact, he opposed the slave trade. Nevertheless, his critics argue that he benefitted from the trade by having it as one of his responsibilities.

It is interesting that Yale's Christian name has two spellings. On his grave it is Eliugh, elsewhere the 'g' is dropped in favour of the biblical Elihu.

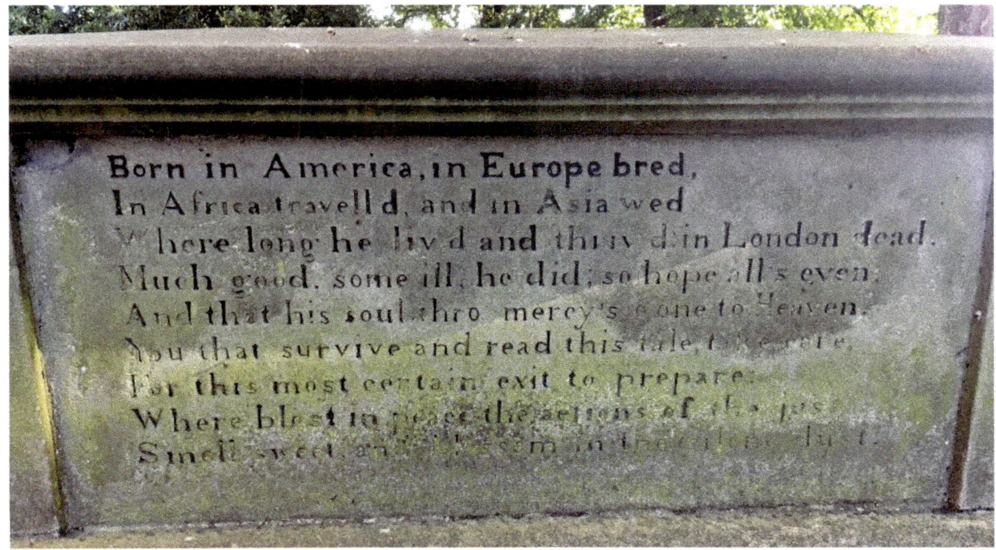

Above: Elihu Yale's tomb in St Giles' churchyard. The lettering on this exposed side of the tomb is becoming eroded. It reads:

Born in Africa, in Europe bred
In Africa travelled and in Asia wed
Where long he lived and thrived, in London dead
Much good, some ill he did, so hope all's even
And that his soul thro mercy's gone to Heaven
You that survive and read this tale take care
For this most certain exit to prepare
Where blest in peace, the actions of the just
Smell sweet and blossom in the silent dust

Below: Yale tomb, St Giles' churchyard.

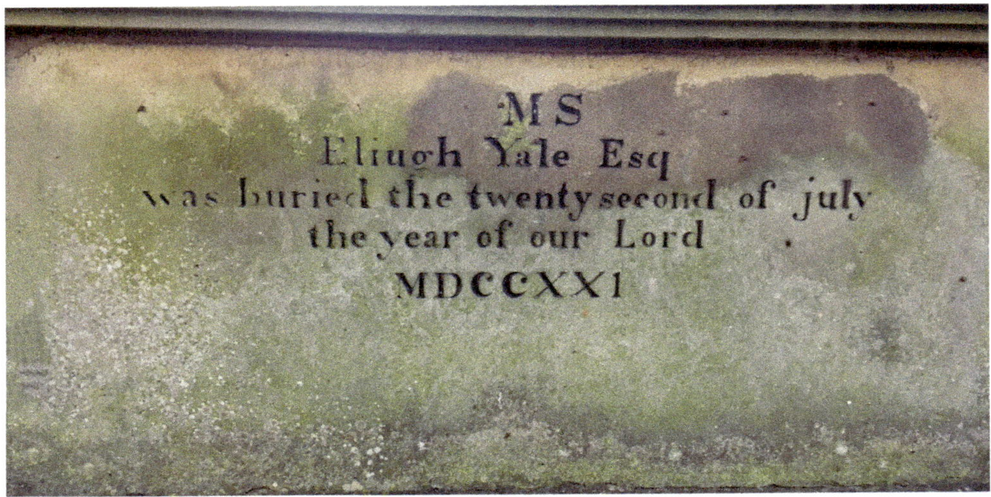

Y Bwa

Y Bwa (The Arc) is the work of the Scottish artist David Annand. It was unveiled by the mayor of Wrexham on 2 February 1996. The sculpture was sponsored by the Welsh Development Agency, the Iron and Steel Trades Confederation, the Arts Council of Wales and WMBC. The two figures depict a steel worker and a coal miner representing the industrial past of the Wrexham area. On the base is a poem by the modern bard Merddyn ap Dafydd of Llanrwst.

Y Bwa

Uwch y waedd, drwy'r gawod chwys – a helynt

Y morthwylion stormus,

Heibio'r awr sy'n bwyta brys

Mae tynfa yma at enfys

The Arc

Above the cry, through streaming sweat – and the storm

Of angry hammers

Past the hour that devours haste

We are drawn towards rainbows

Y Bwa (The Arc). The work of the Scottish artist David Annand, the two figures represent a steel worker and a miner.

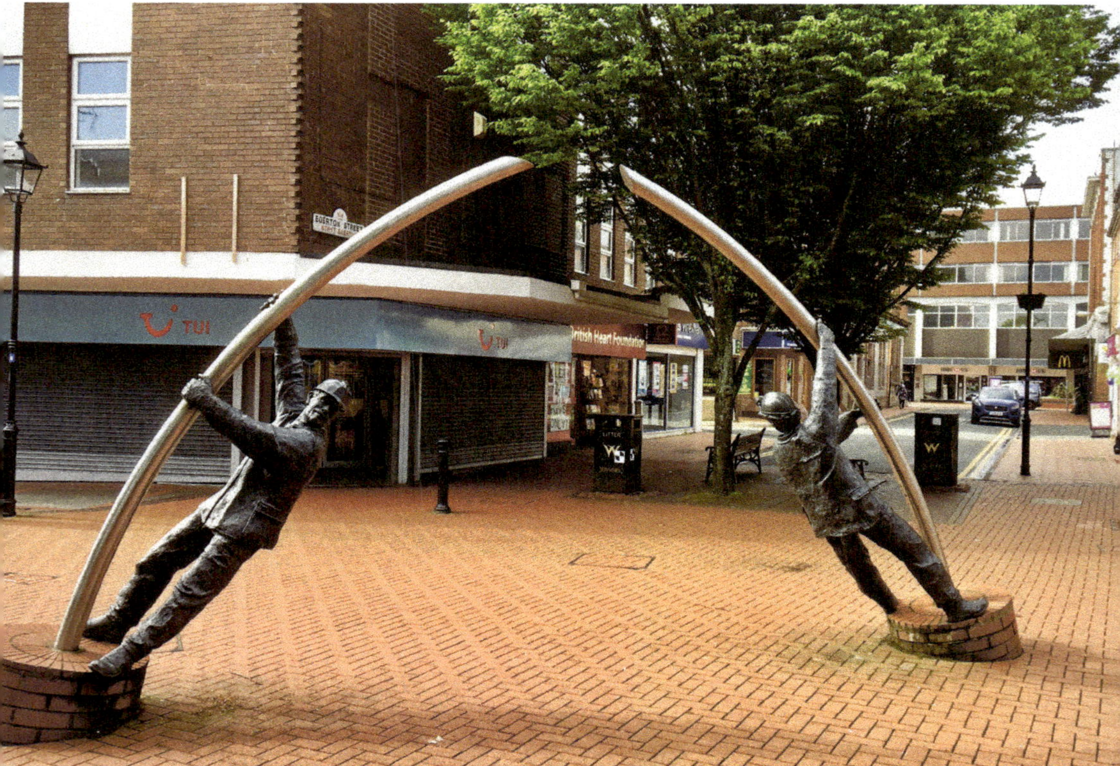

Zoedone Mineral Works

As the letter Z is rarely used in Welsh, I was concerned that I would find nothing in Wrexham to fit under this letter. Then I found a reference to the Zoedone Mineral Works. This company was established in the 1880s and was based in Pentre Felin. In the next decade, it was renamed the Aereated Beverage Buffet Company. Recently, one of the company's mineral water bottles was offered for sale on eBay.

Acknowledgements

The author wishes to acknowledge the help and advice given by the staff of Denbighshire Record Office and that of his friends in Wrexham for their help and suggestions. Particular thanks to Diane Powell for reading through the first draft and making some useful suggestions.

About the Author

Christopher Davies has been involved in local history research for over forty years. During that time, he has written a number of books and guides. His particular interest is in seventeenth-century history, but he also has a strong interest in industrial history, particularly as it relates to railways and canals. He has studied history at both Leicester and Cambridge universities and is a Fellow of the Royal Historical Society. Now retired, he was professionally engaged in adult education and training. He currently lives in Trevor.